The Etudes Project
Vol. 1: ICEBERG

Curated by Jenny Lin

NewMusicShelf
www.newmusicshelf.com

NEWMUSICSHELF, INC.

Published in the United States of America
by NewMusicShelf, Inc.
34-29 32nd St., 3rd floor, Astoria, NY 11106
www.newmusicshelf.com

Copyright © 2019 by NewMusicShelf, Inc.

First printing 2019

Contents

Introduction.. v
Performance Notes vii

Drake Andersen: Walk (2018) 1

Victor Báez: Étude No. 1: Corona (2018) 6

Stephanie Ann Boyd: Lilac (2018) 12
    from Flower Catalog

Alex Burtzos: Should the Wide World Roll Away (2018) 18

Yu-Chun Chien: To the Convergence (2018) 28

Derek Cooper: Etude No. 1: Unleashed (2018)... 31

Max Grafe: Accretion (2018) 40

Will Healy: Etudes for Melancholy Robots: III (2018) 44

Jonathan Russ: Knuckles (2018) 56

Harry Stafylakis: Obstinata 1: Barbed Wire (2018)...................................... 64
    from Piano Études, Book I

About the Curator... 77
About the Composers.. 78
Supplementary Material 88

INTRODUCTION

The Etudes Project is an ongoing exploration of the tradition and transformation of keyboard virtuosity in the piano repertoire. Inspired by my world tour of Philip Glass' *Piano Etudes* with the composer himself, I created the Etudes Project with the idea juxtaposing new works alongside some of the most challenging works from the existing piano etudes repertoire.

To inaugurate this project, I have partnered with ICEBERG New Music, a collective of 10 composers based in New York City, to create a program of new solo piano etudes that run the stylistic gamut from pop-inspired dance music to avant-garde constructions. Each of these pieces has been paired with an existing etude – by Chopin, Rachmaninoff, Debussy, Scriabin, Crawford Seeger, Messiaen, Ligeti, Glass, Chin, and Hosokawa, – inviting listeners to search for connections between virtuosic piano writing from the past and present. The entire collection of Etudes have been recorded and are available on the Sono Luminus label and all the new ICEBERG Etudes are published here by NewMusicShelf, making these exciting works available to future generations.

I am deeply grateful to Alex Burtzos, founder of ICEBERG New Music, as well as all the composers - Derek, Drake, Harry, Jon, Max, Stephanie, Viktor, Will, Yu-Chun - for taking on this project with me, and to Dennis from NewMusicShelf for his tremendous effort in giving this music a permanent home.

— Jenny Lin

PERFORMANCE NOTES

Jonathan Russ: Knuckles

Knuckles explores the textures and timbres of house music piano, drawing in particular from the work of legendary producer Frankie Knuckles.

Rhythms should be as close to metronomically accurate as possible, but always with an ear towards maintaining propulsive energy.

Tempos may be adjusted per the needs of the performer and the room (q=116 is not strictly necessary). Small tempo changes are acceptable at the beginnings of new sections, and subtle accel / rit may be used as needed; these adjustments should not be overly dramatic, serving primarily to highlight the character of each section and to allow for performer comfort.

for Jenny Lin

Walk

after Scriabin, Op. 65 No. 1

DRAKE ANDERSEN
(2018)

Allegro fantastico (♩ = 108)

f

ff

*minimal pedal throughout
(unless otherwise indicated)*

Senza misura

Begin very slowly and softly

Single, long accelerando over all repeats (to each ♩ as ♪ at ♩ = 108)

Repeat 3 or 4 times. On repeats, can improvise variations in note order, create chords, etc.

accel. ....

(attacca)

pp * --- *f*

Ped. ad lib.

★ Single, long cresc. over all repeates from *pp* to *f*

A tempo (♩ = 108)

p sub.

mp

p

mf

7
p sub.
sfz
ff
10
mf
f
p sub.
13
ff
mf
p
ad lib. to approx. ♪ = 60
17
3
ff
l.v.
pp
mp

A tempo (♩ = 108)
marcato
20
pp
p
sf
24
p sub.
mf
p sub.
28
f
p
mf
p sub.
32
(♪ = ♪)
f
p sub.

(♪ = ♪)
36
f
39
p sub.
poco rit.
mf
p
Ped.
Ped.
blur with Ped.
5
A tempo (♩ = 108)
marcato, as before
43
mf
mp
46
f
p sub.
mf
p sub.

accented notes in rilievo
49
mf
p sub.
ff
pp
sf
52
55
(♪ = ♪)
ff sub.
59
pp sub.
64
p sub.
fff

Étude No. 1

Corona

VÍCTOR BÁEZ
(2018)

In strict tempo (♩ = 180)

cresc. poco a poco to m. 29

absolutely no pedal throughout the entire piece

the repeated notes are to be played in a continuous, regular, and precise fashion,
without any accents other than those specifically indicated

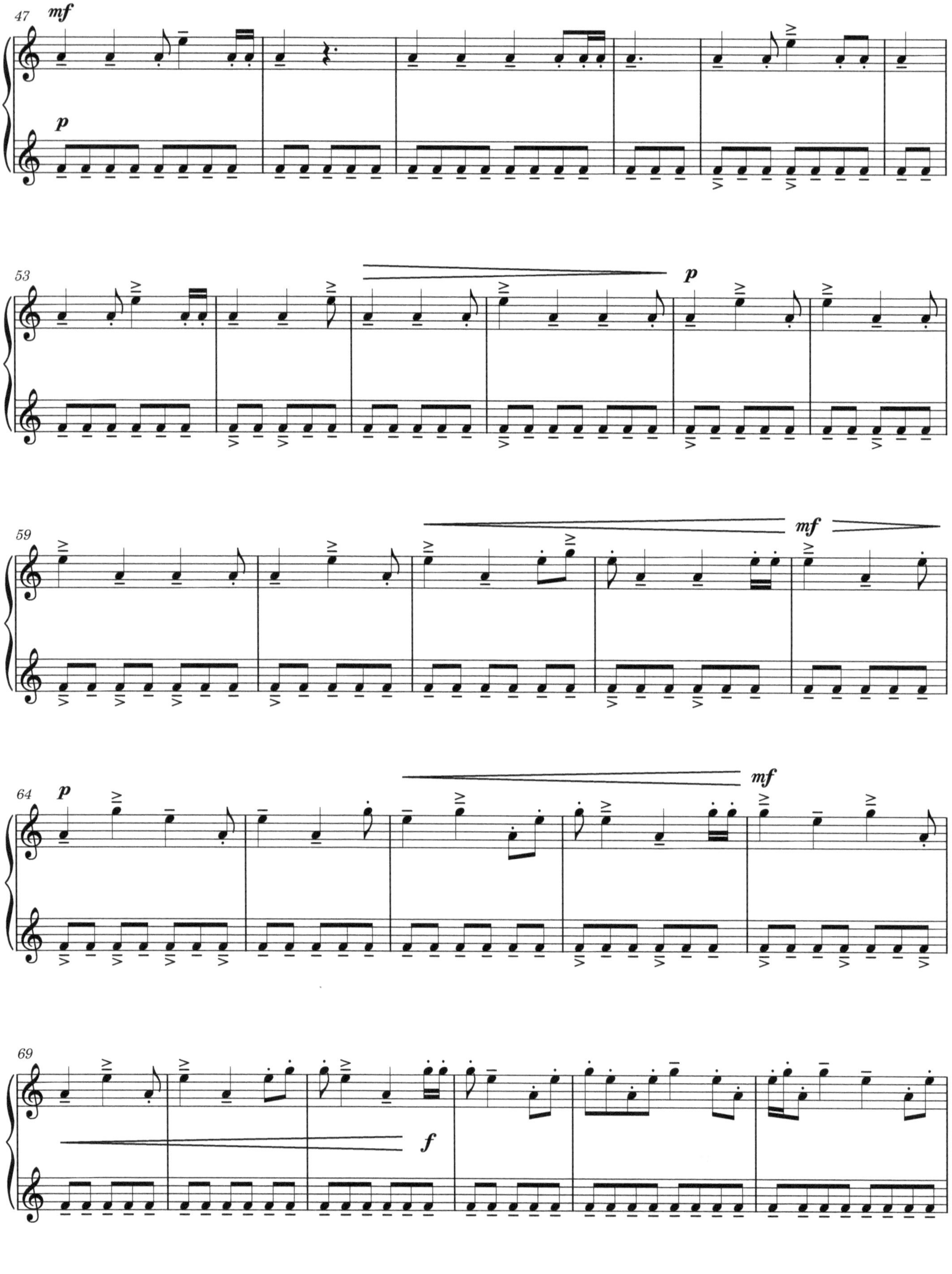
47
mf
p
53
p
59
mf
64
p
mf
69
f

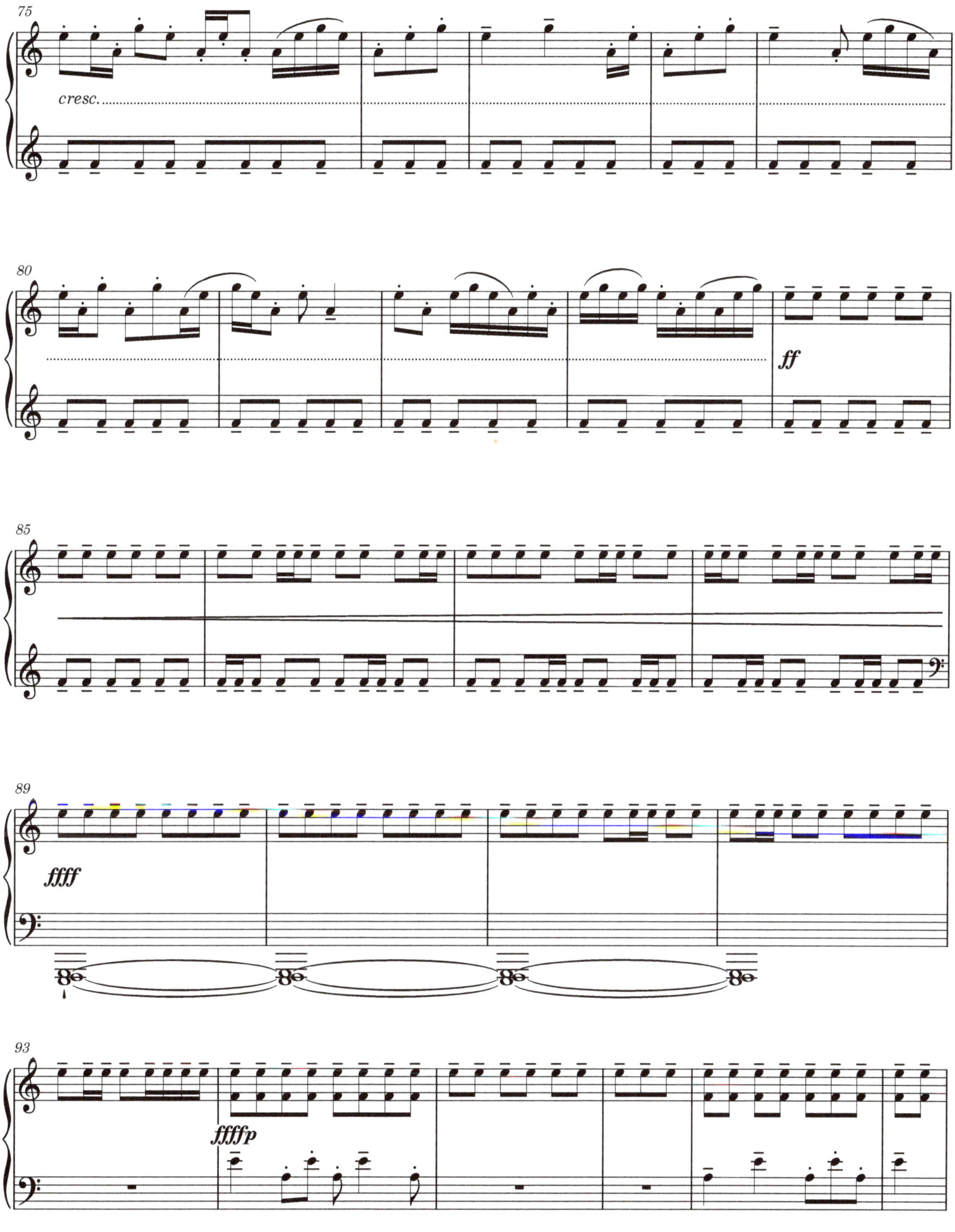
75
cresc.
80
ff
85
89
ffff
93
ffffp

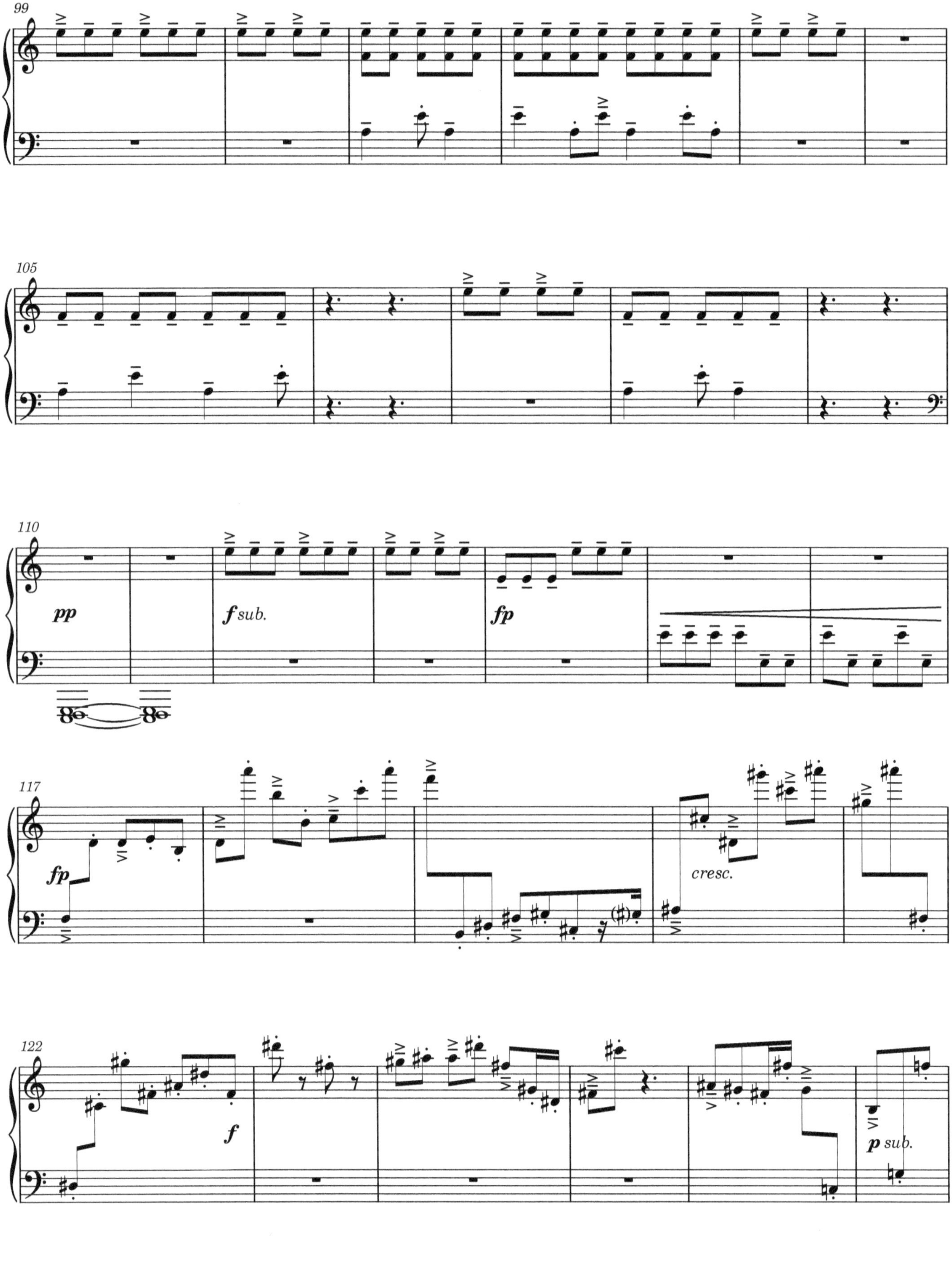
99
105
110
pp
f sub.
fp
117
fp
cresc.
122
f
p sub.

*key pizz.: lift the key vertically upwards from its front edge, then let it go.

Commissioned by and written for Jenny Lin

Lilac

from Flower Catalog

STEPHANIE ANN BOYD
(2018)

Perfumed, translucent; fragments of memory (♩ = 92)

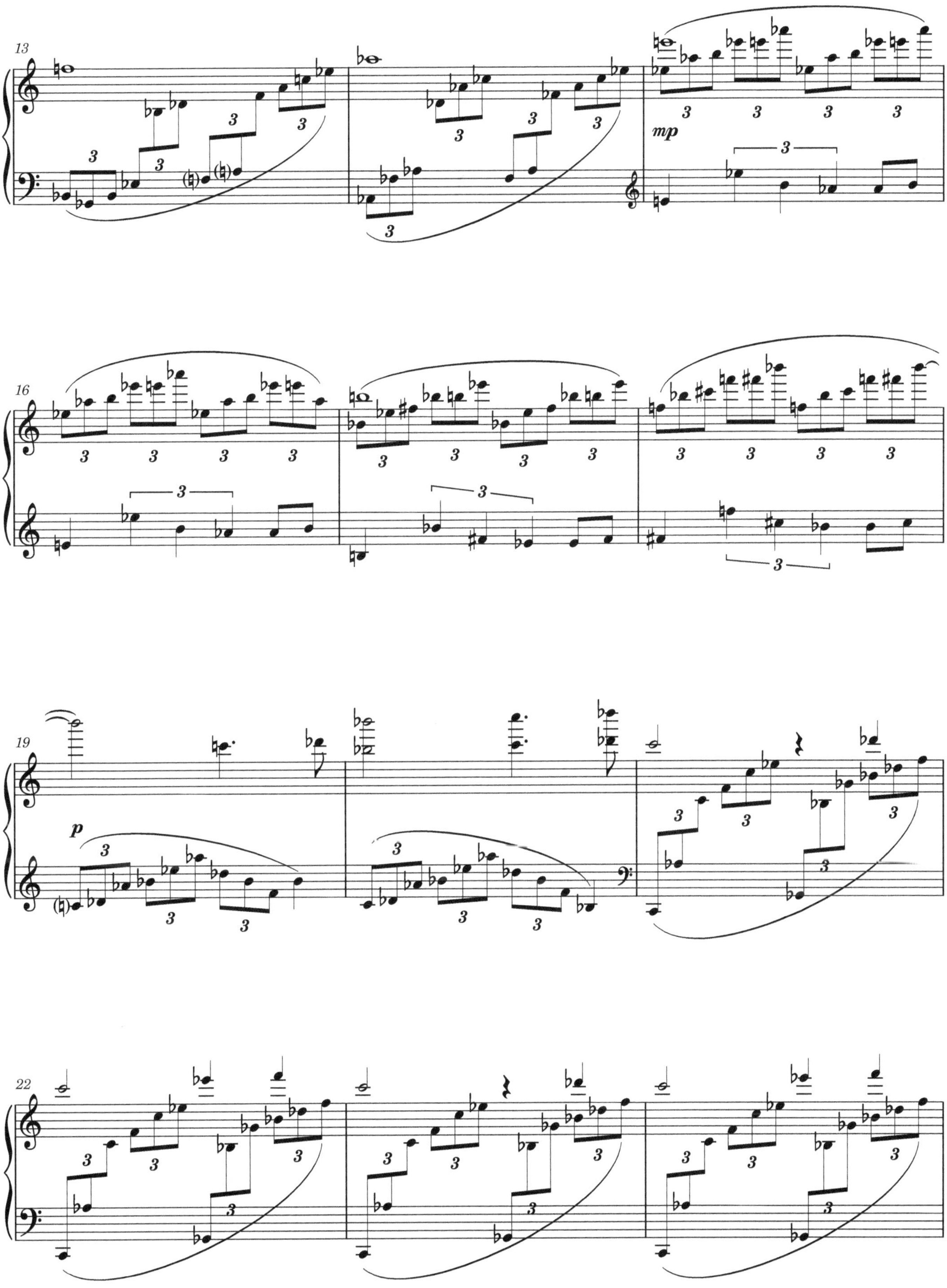
13
mp
16
19
p
22

Warm, with momentum

Reeling...

Dizzying; mesmerized

pedal to let resonance naturally blur into next two measures

pedal to let resonance naturally blur into next two measures

pedal to let resonance naturally blur into next two measures

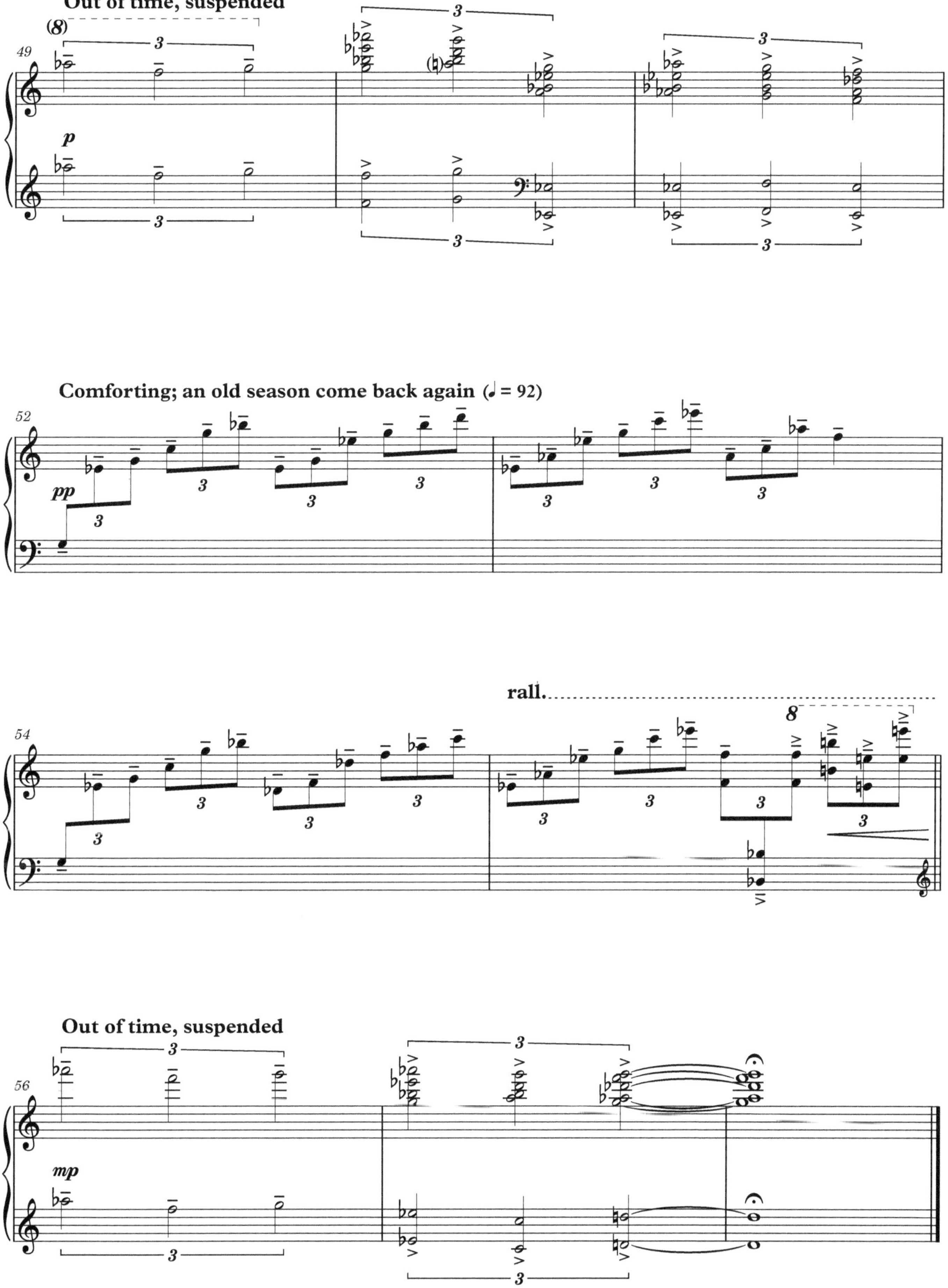
Out of time, suspended
p
Comforting; an old season come back again (♩ = 92)
pp
rall.
Out of time, suspended
mp

for Jenny Lin
Should the Wide World Roll Away
(Étude)

ALEX BURTZOS
(2018)

12
pp
16
mf
19
f
mf
f
mf
22
blurry until m. 26
pp sub.
Ped.
24
mf
pp
8
(Ped.)

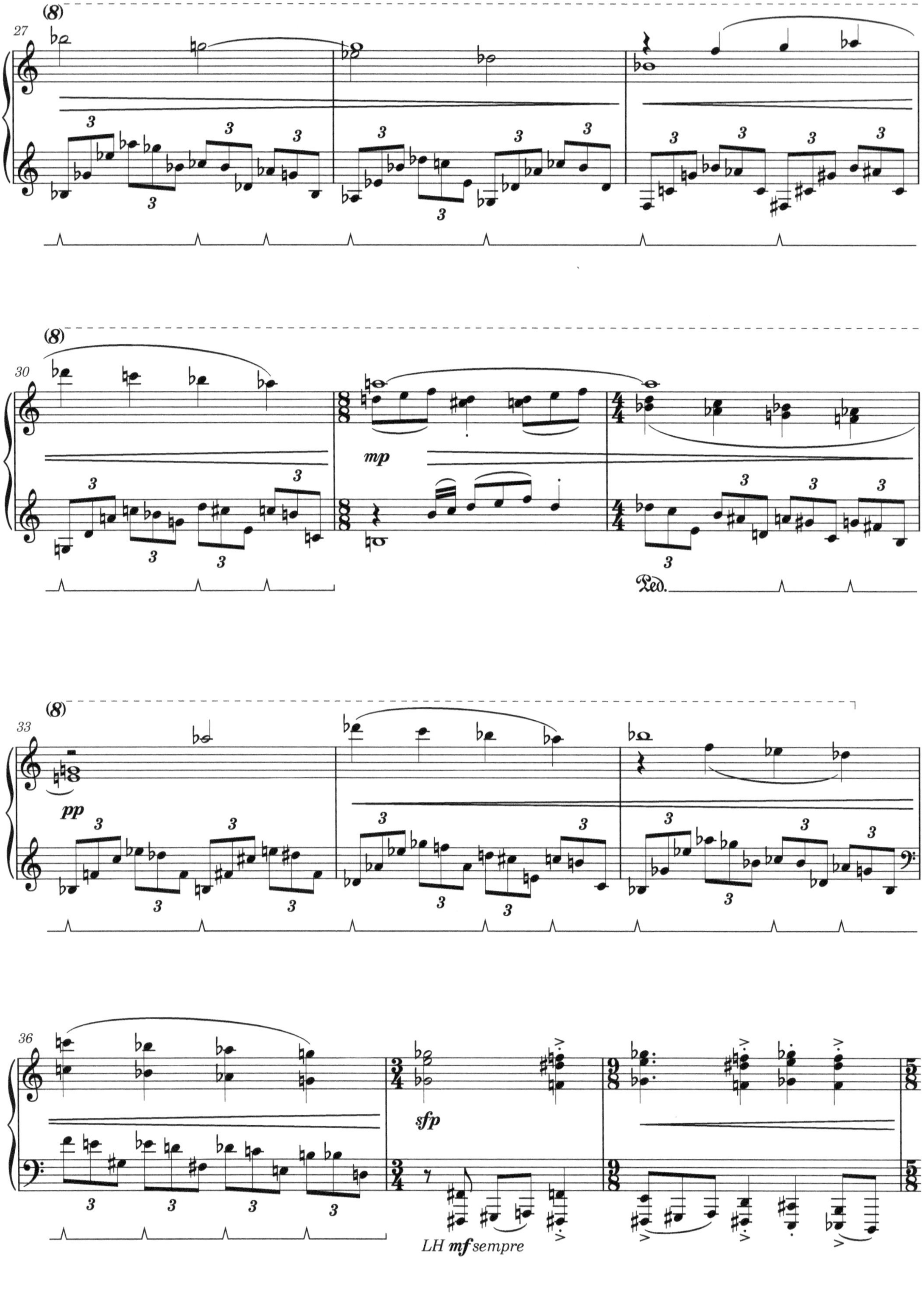
(8)
mp
Ped.
pp
sfp
LH mf sempre

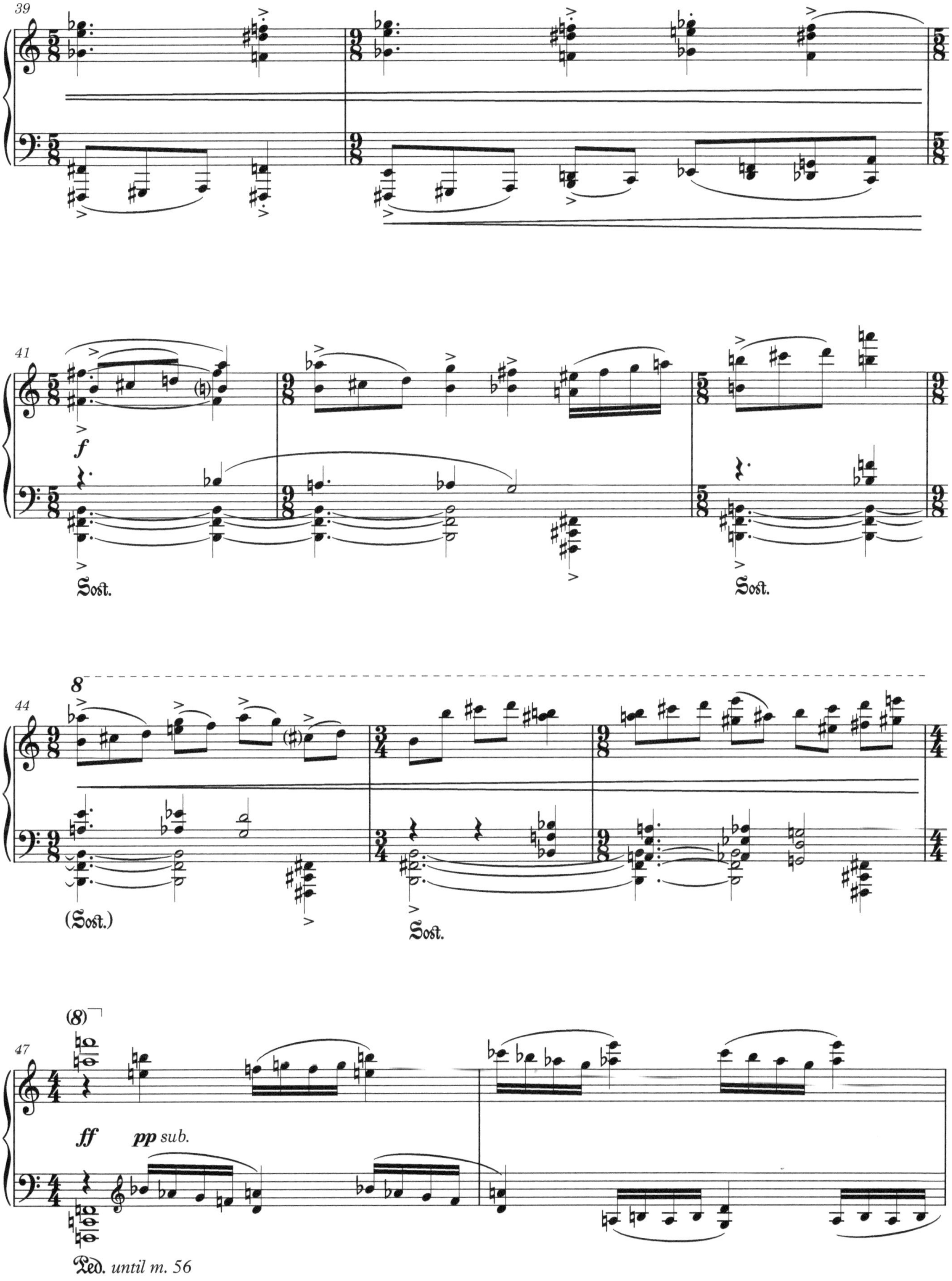
f
Sost.
Sost.
(Sost.)
Sost.
ff
pp sub.
Ped. until m. 56

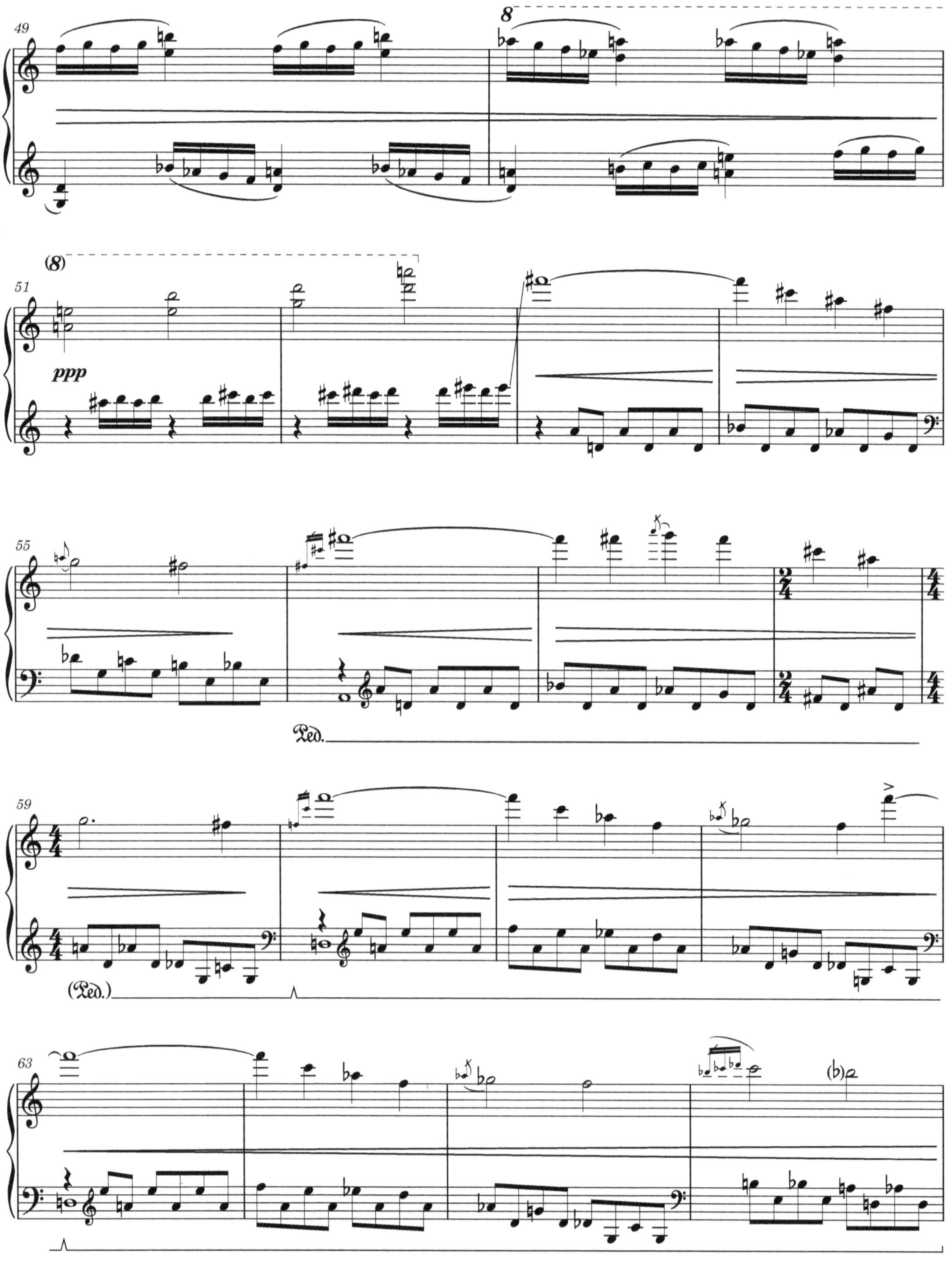
49
8
(8)
51
ppp
55
Ped.
59
(Ped.)
63

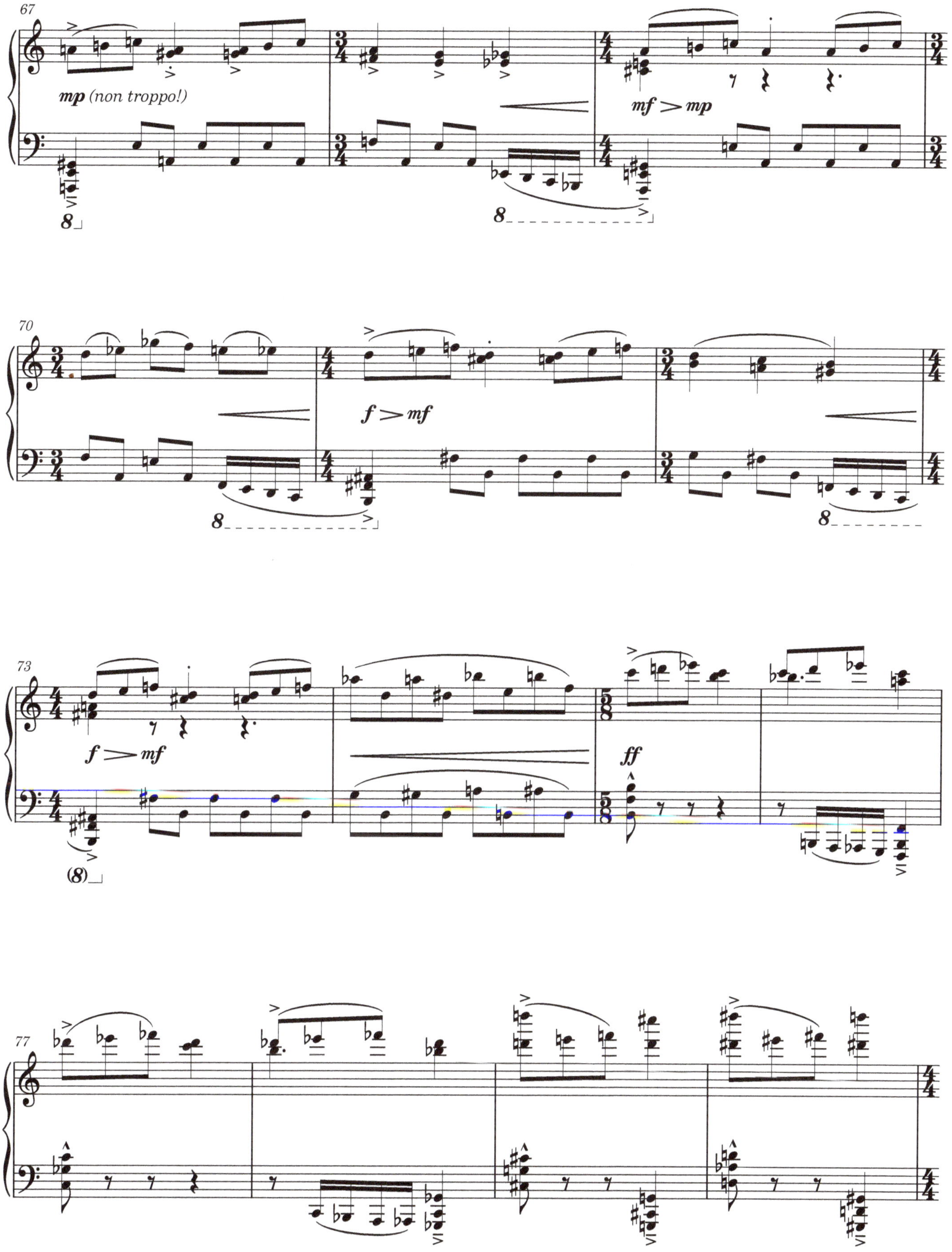
67
mp (non troppo!)
mf > mp
70
f > mf
73
f > mf
ff
77

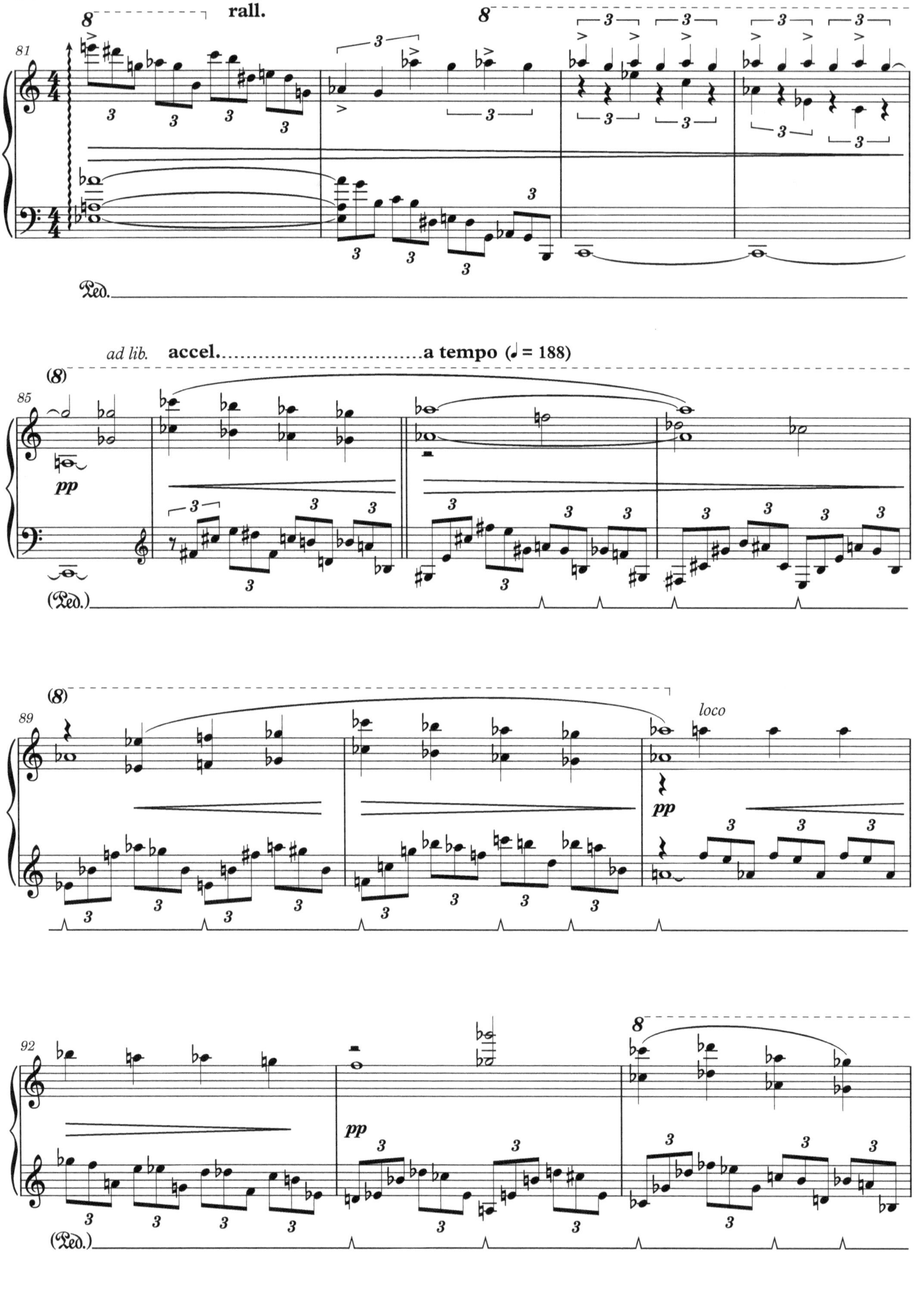
rall.
ad lib.
accel.................................a tempo (♩ = 188)
loco
pp
Ped.
(Ped.)

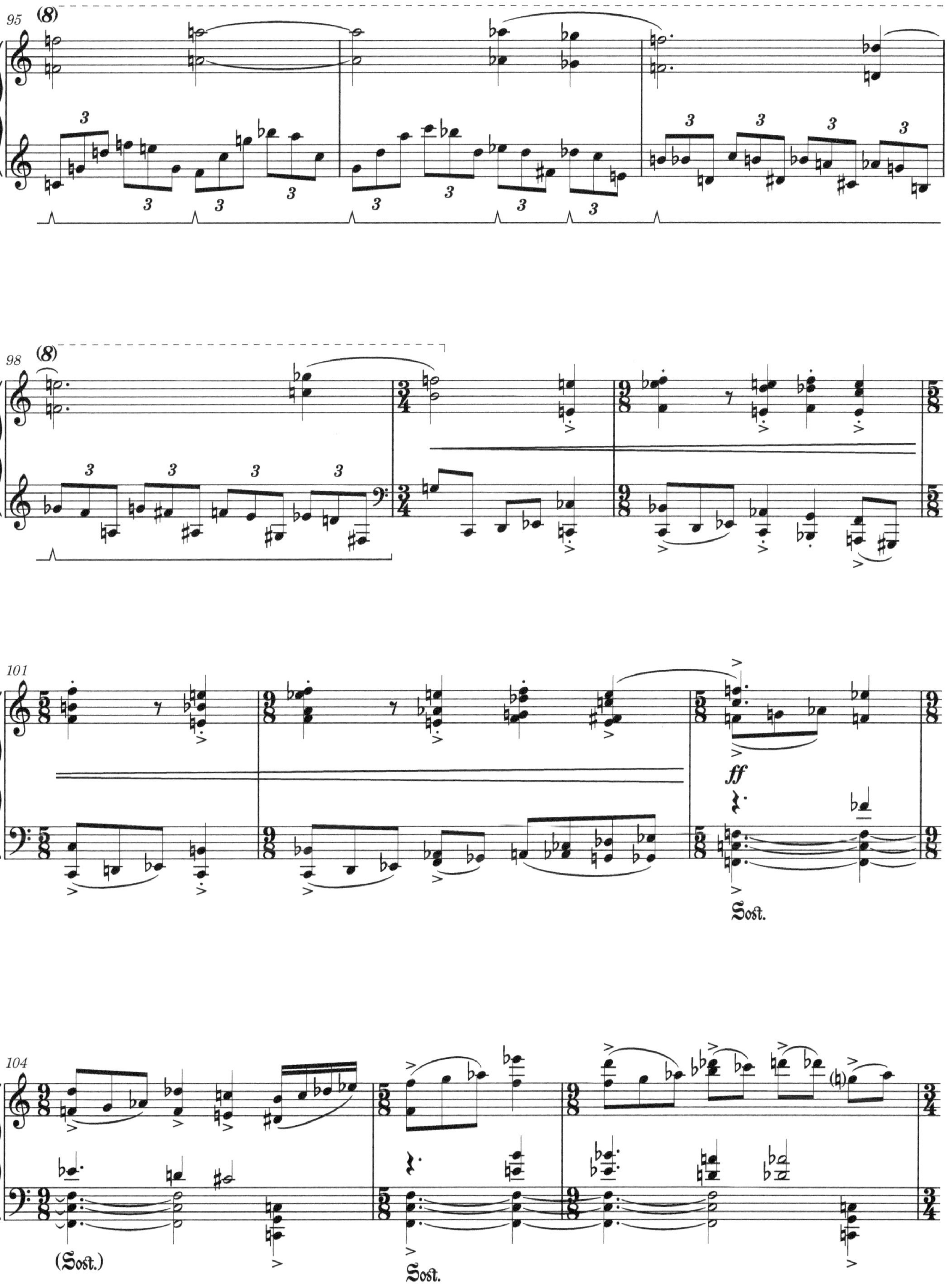
95
(8)
98
(8)
101
ff
Sost.
104
(Sost.)
Sost.

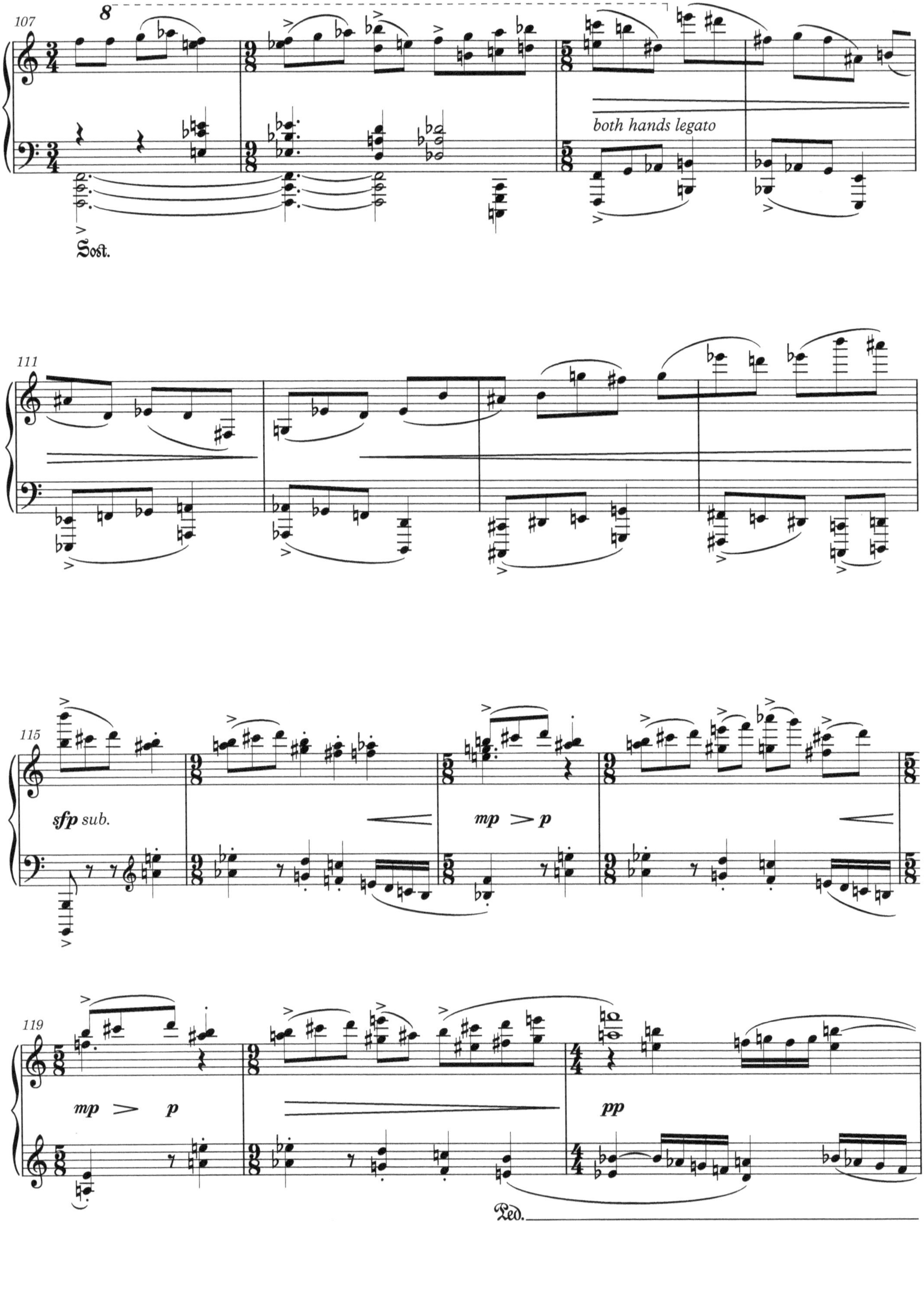
107
8
both hands legato
Sost.
111
115
sfp sub.
mp > p
119
mp > p
pp
Ped.

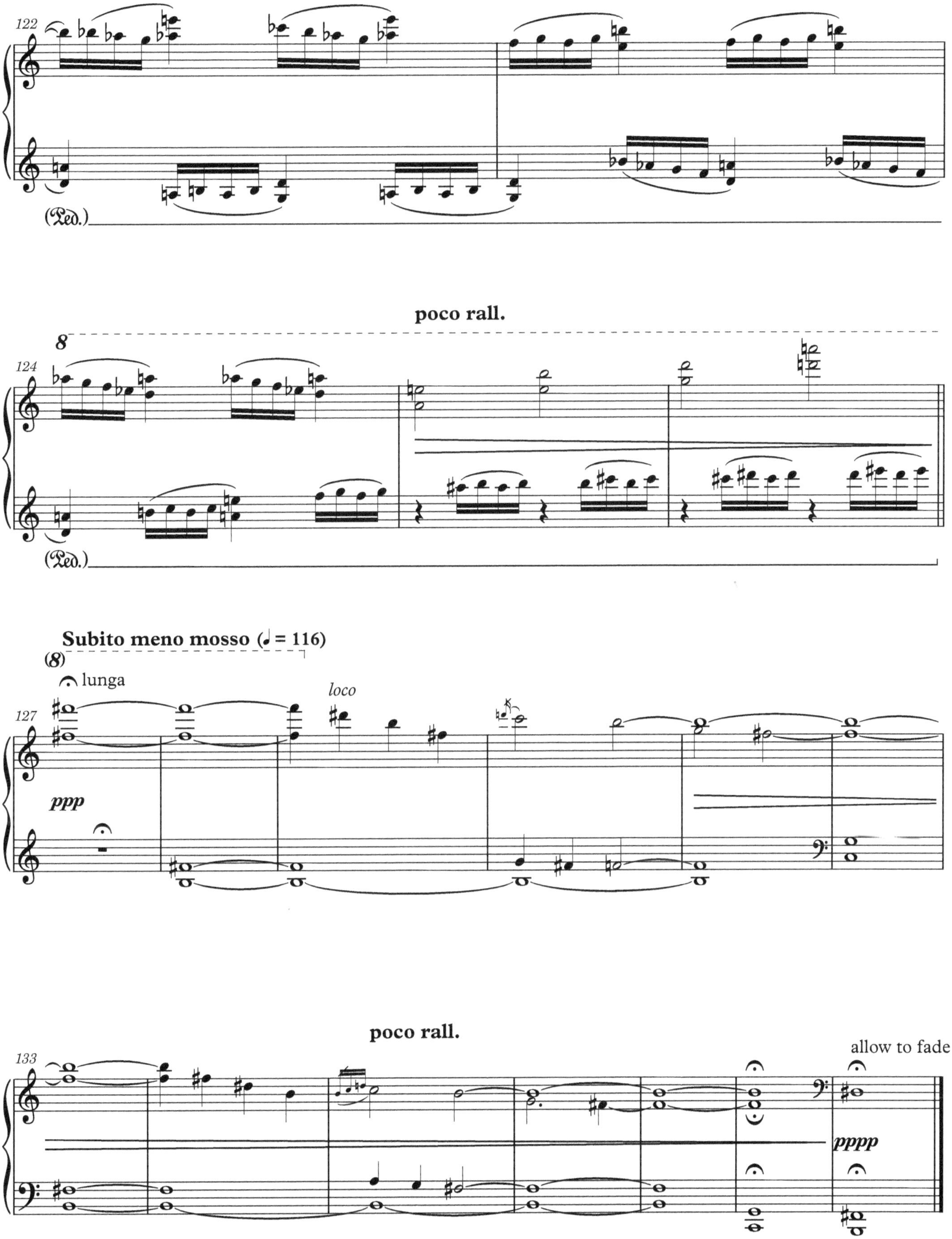
122
(Ped.)
poco rall.
8
124
(Ped.)
Subito meno mosso (♩ = 116)
(8)
lunga
127
loco
ppp
poco rall.
133
allow to fade
pppp

To the Convergence

YU-CHUN CHIEN
(2018)

(8)
(Ped.)
(8)
mf
p f p
tr (slowly→fast)
fp f p
mf
pp
gradually change
f con fuoco

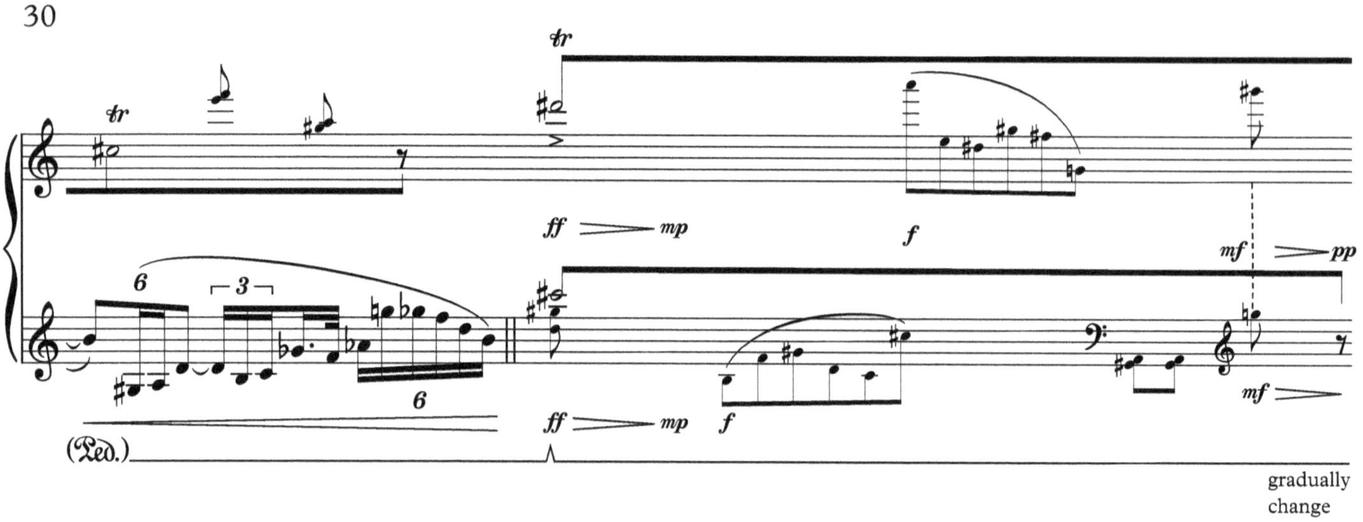
tr
ff mp
f
mf pp
6
3
6
ff mp
f
mf
(Ped.)
gradually
change

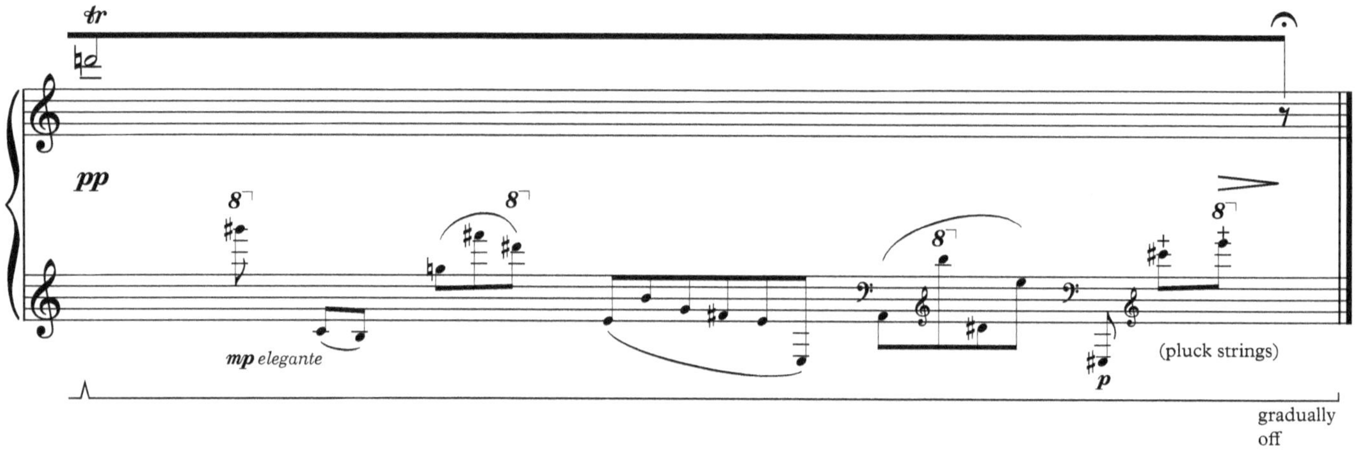
tr
pp
8
mp elegante
(pluck strings)
p
gradually
off

for pianist Jenny Lin

Etude No. 1

Unleashed

DEREK COOPER
(2018)

Aggressively Presto (♩. = 180)

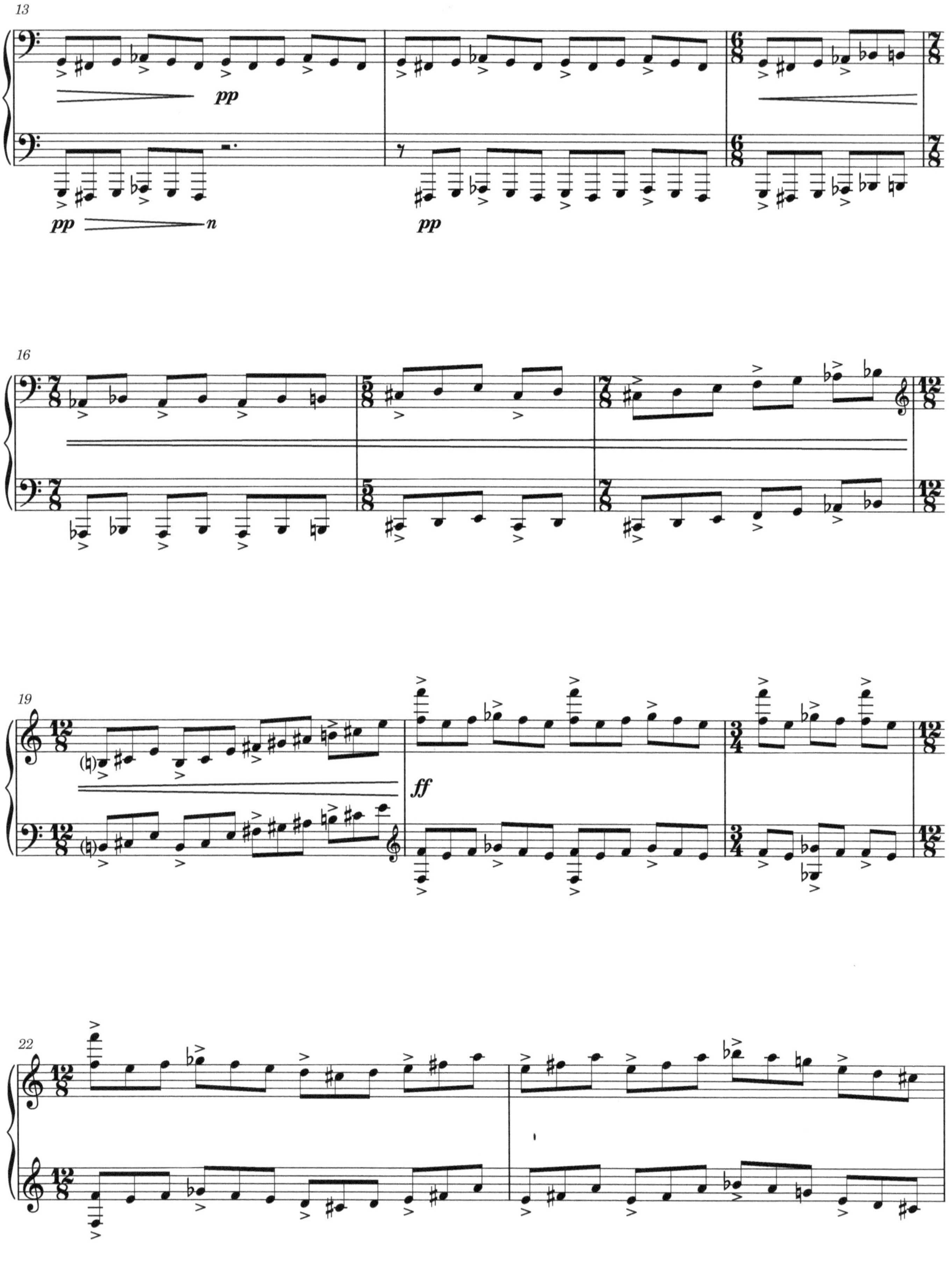
13
pp
pp
n
pp
16
19
ff
22

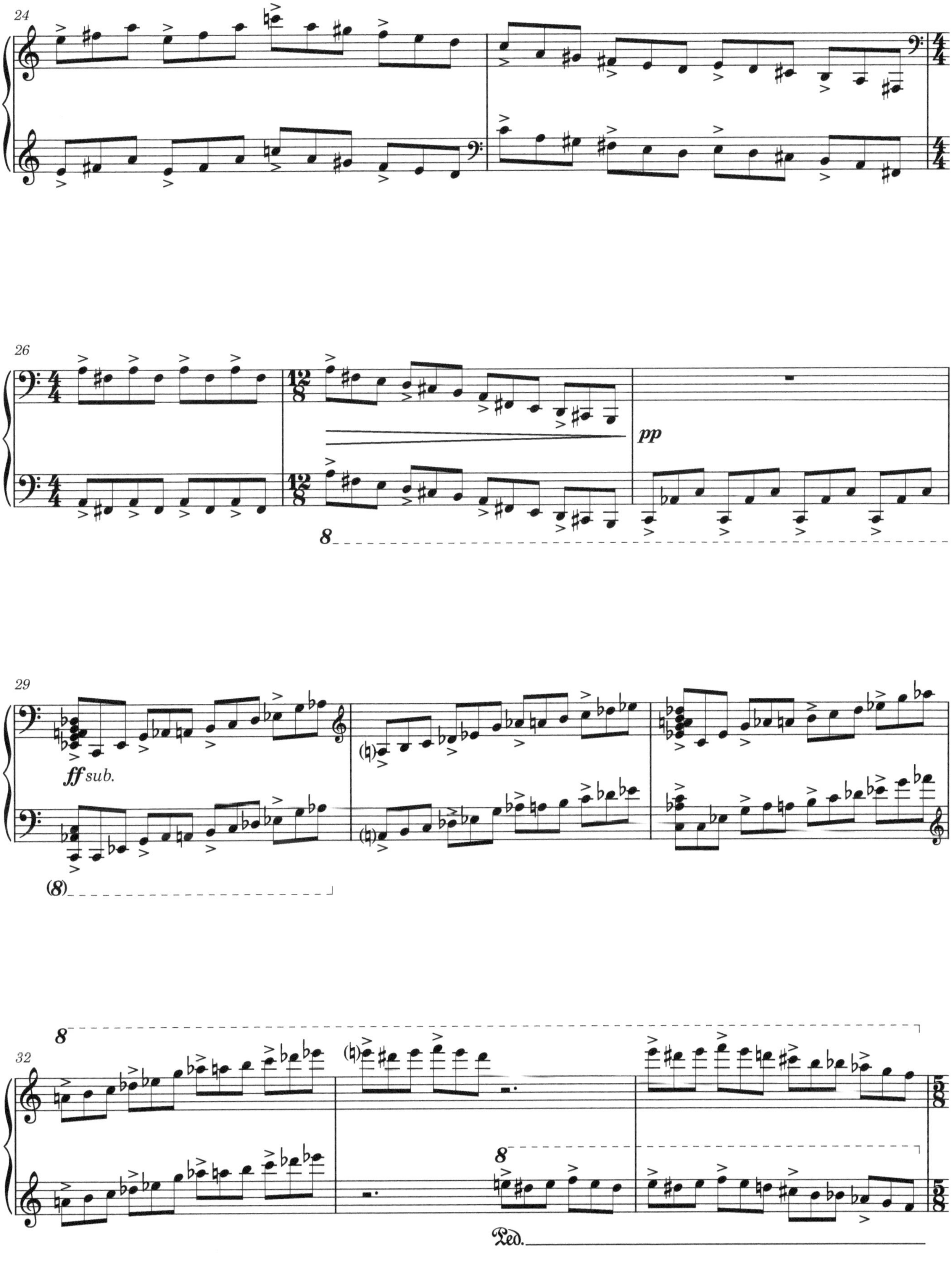
24
26
pp
8
29
ff sub.
(8)
32
8
8
Ped.

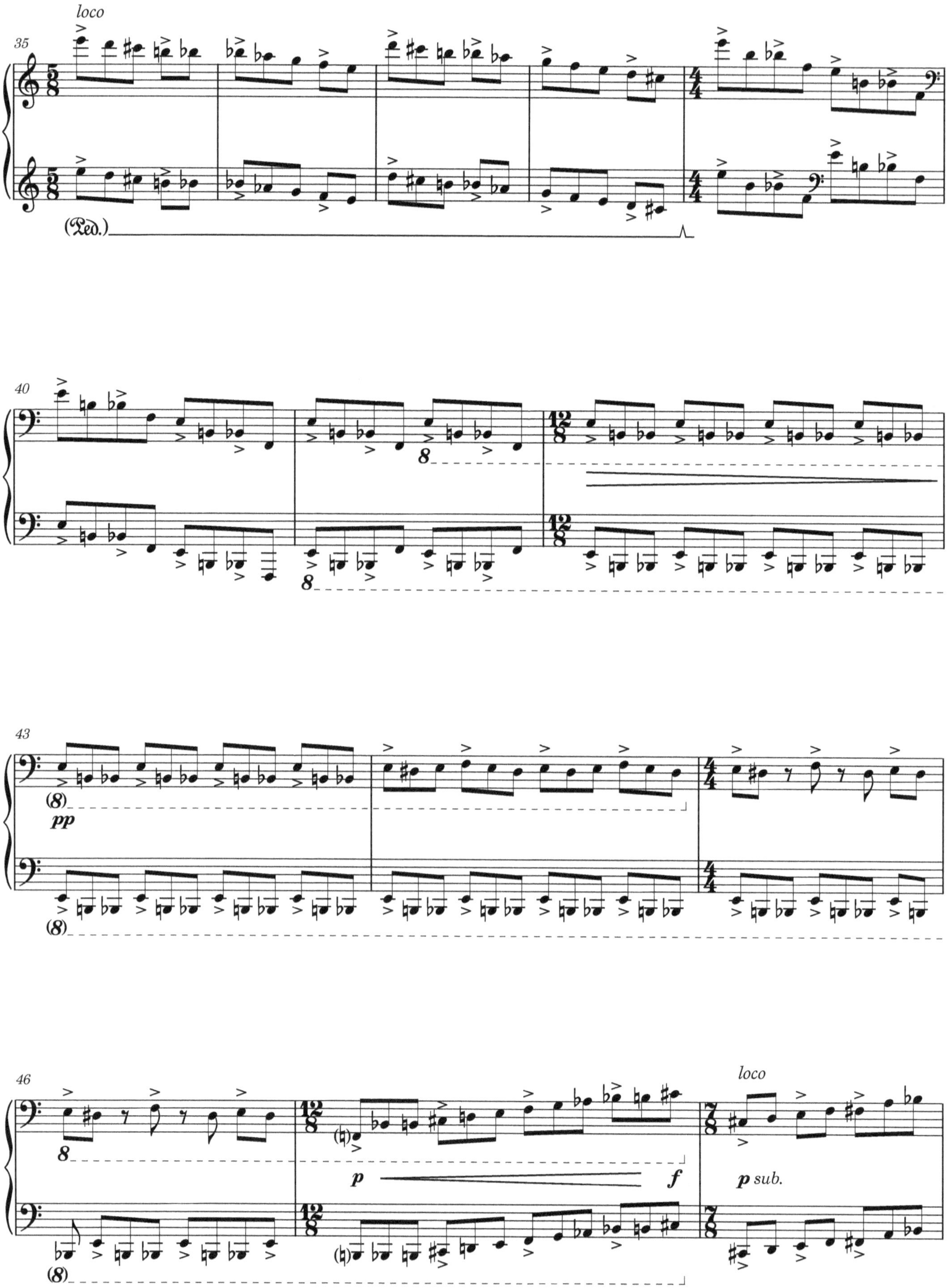
loco
35
(Ped.)
40
8
43
(8)
pp
46
p
f
loco
p sub.

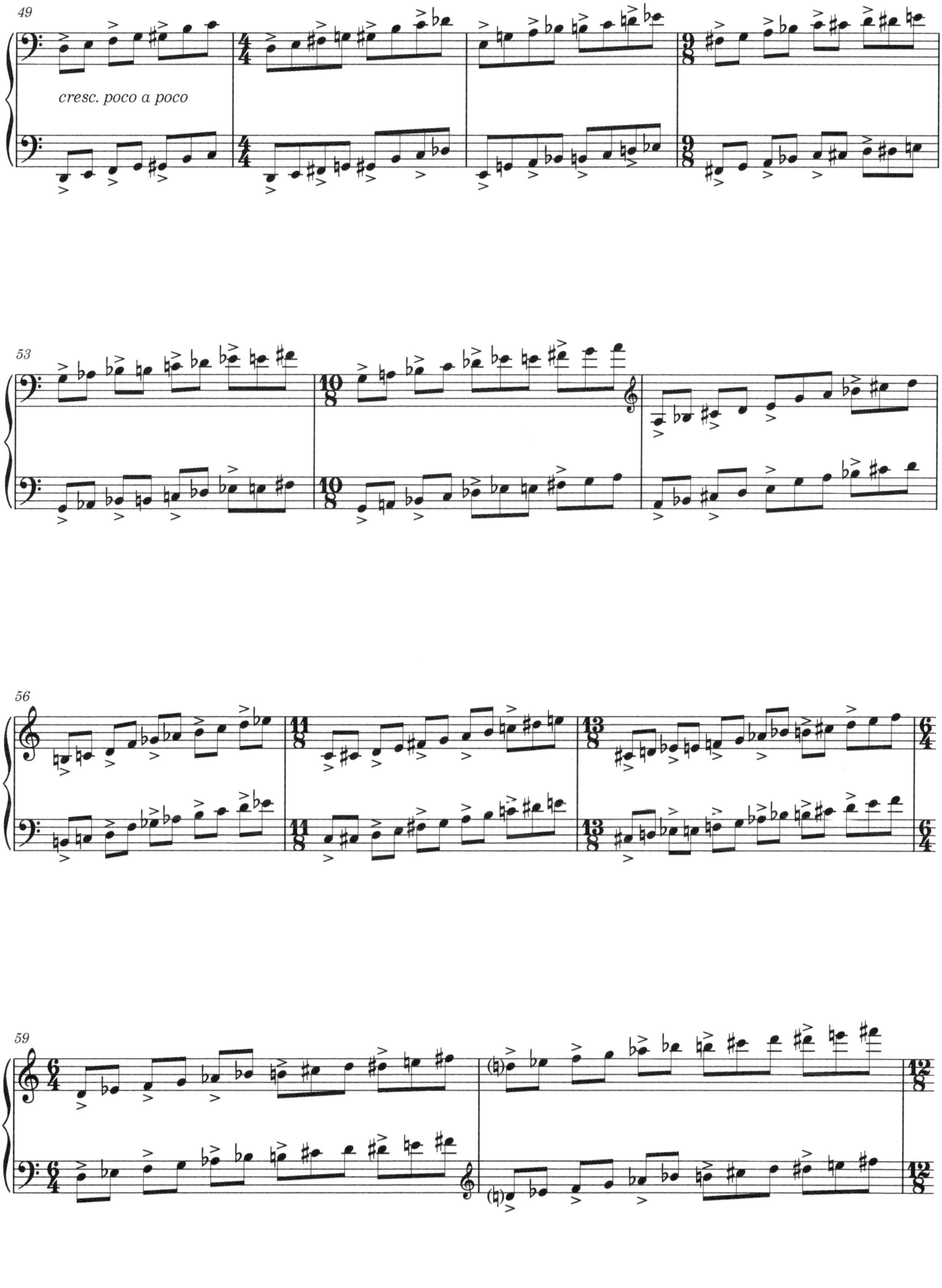
49
cresc. poco a poco
53
56
59

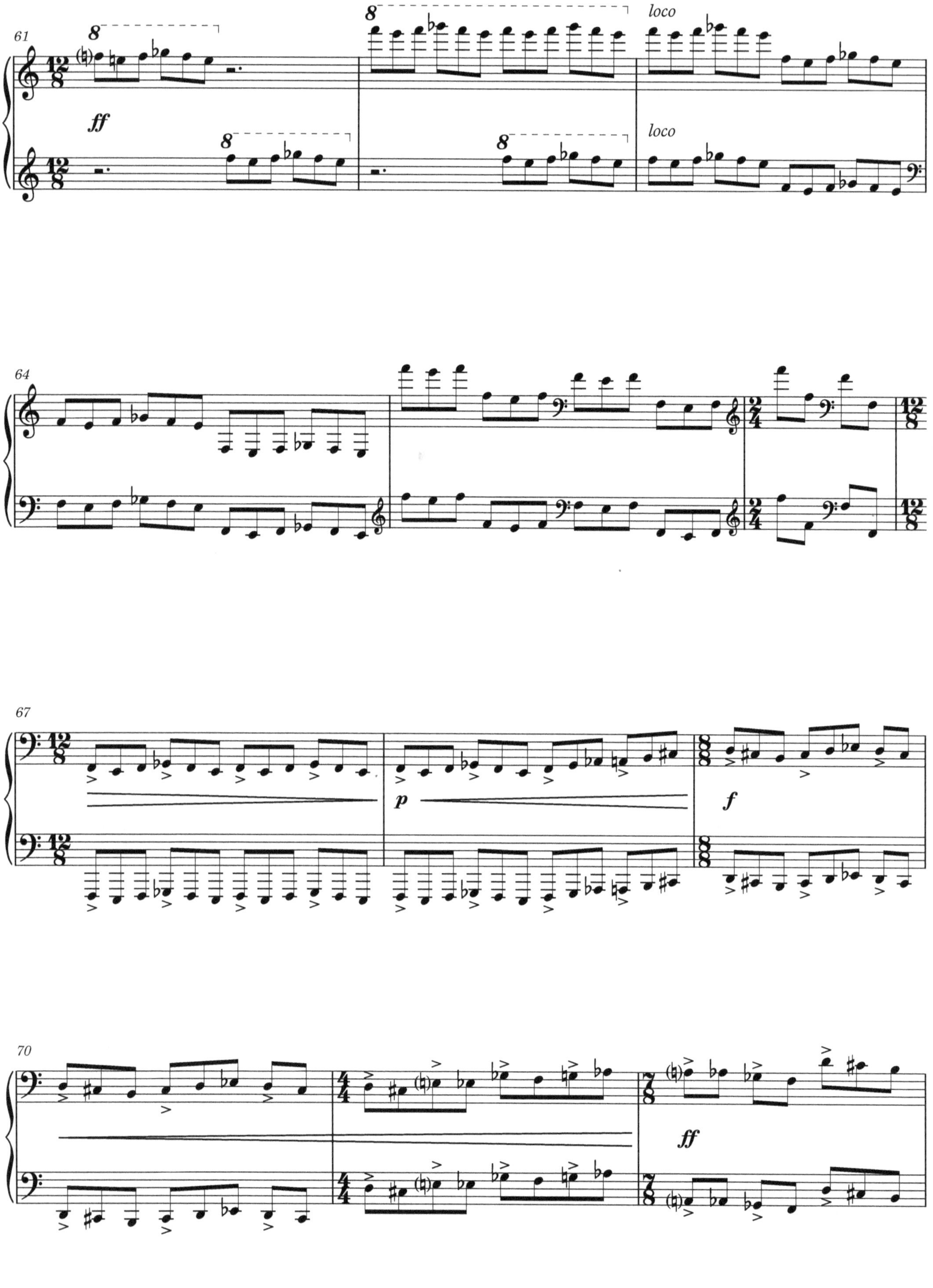
61
8
ff
loco
64
67
p
f
70
ff

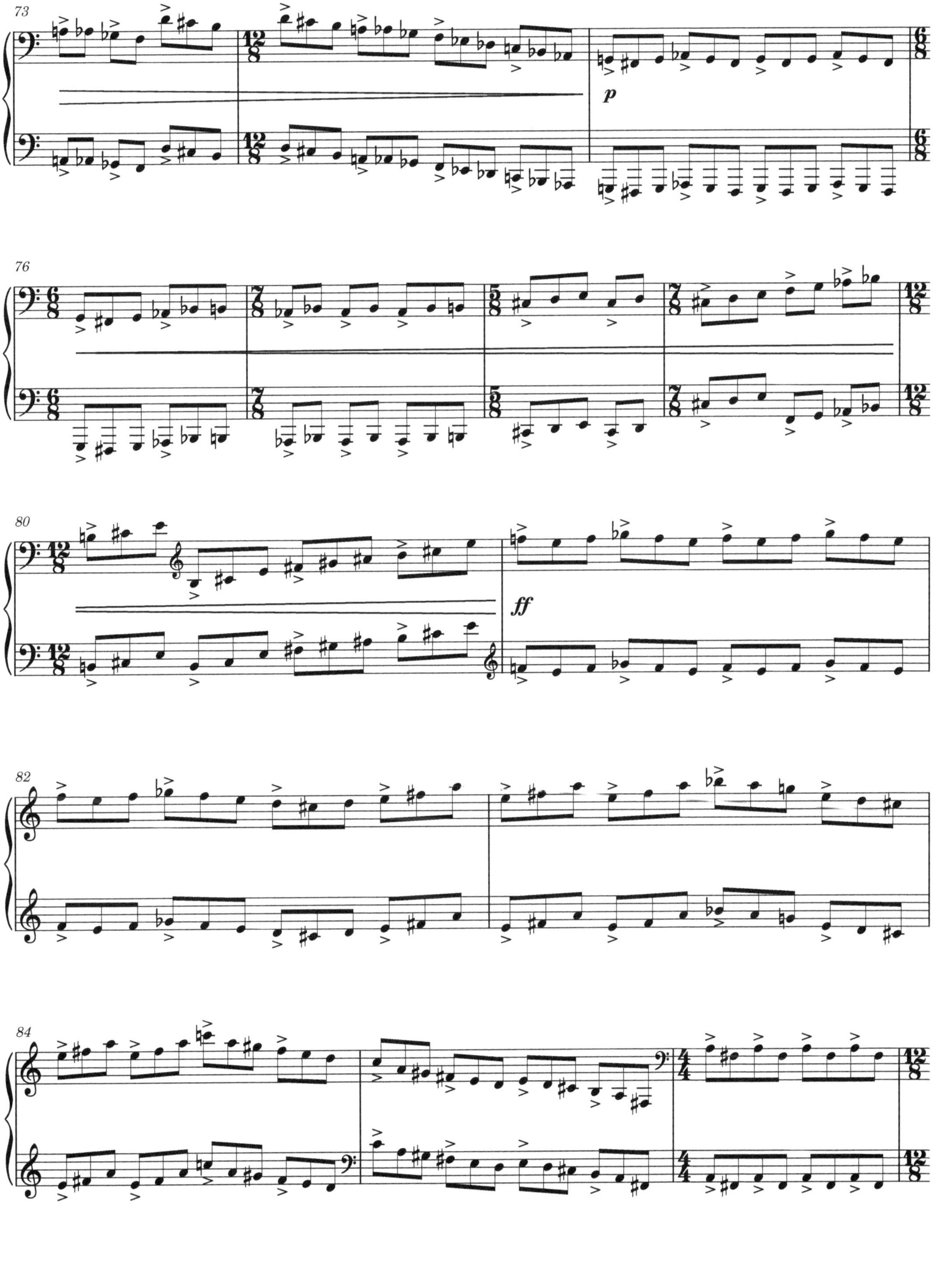
73
p
76
80
ff
82
84

Feel free to stretch tempo as needed, but also
take the opportunity to enjoy the challenge

Let ring as long as posible with pedal

for Jenny Lin

Accretion

study for piano

MAX GRAFE
(2018)

A **Tranquil, bell-like (poco rubato)** (♪ = 76)

p sempre

mf sempre

pp sempre

Ped.

* All grace notes very fast and before the beat

2nd time only

(Ped.)

Ped.

B **Extremely fast, robotically steady**

★★   c. 8"

r l r l etc.

(continue repeated notes)

pp sempre

n

mf

f

mp

Ped.

** The number of repetitions of notes without noteheads in indefinite; duration is proportional to horizontal spacing

repeat pattern in parentheses

pp sempre

fff sub. , frenzied melodramatic

Ped.

pp

pp

Jittery, off-kilter (giusto) (♩= 76)
accel. poco a poco
secchissimo
mf secchissimo
ppp possibile (nearly inaudible)
cresc. poco a poco al fine...
♩= 88 accel. poco a poco
loco

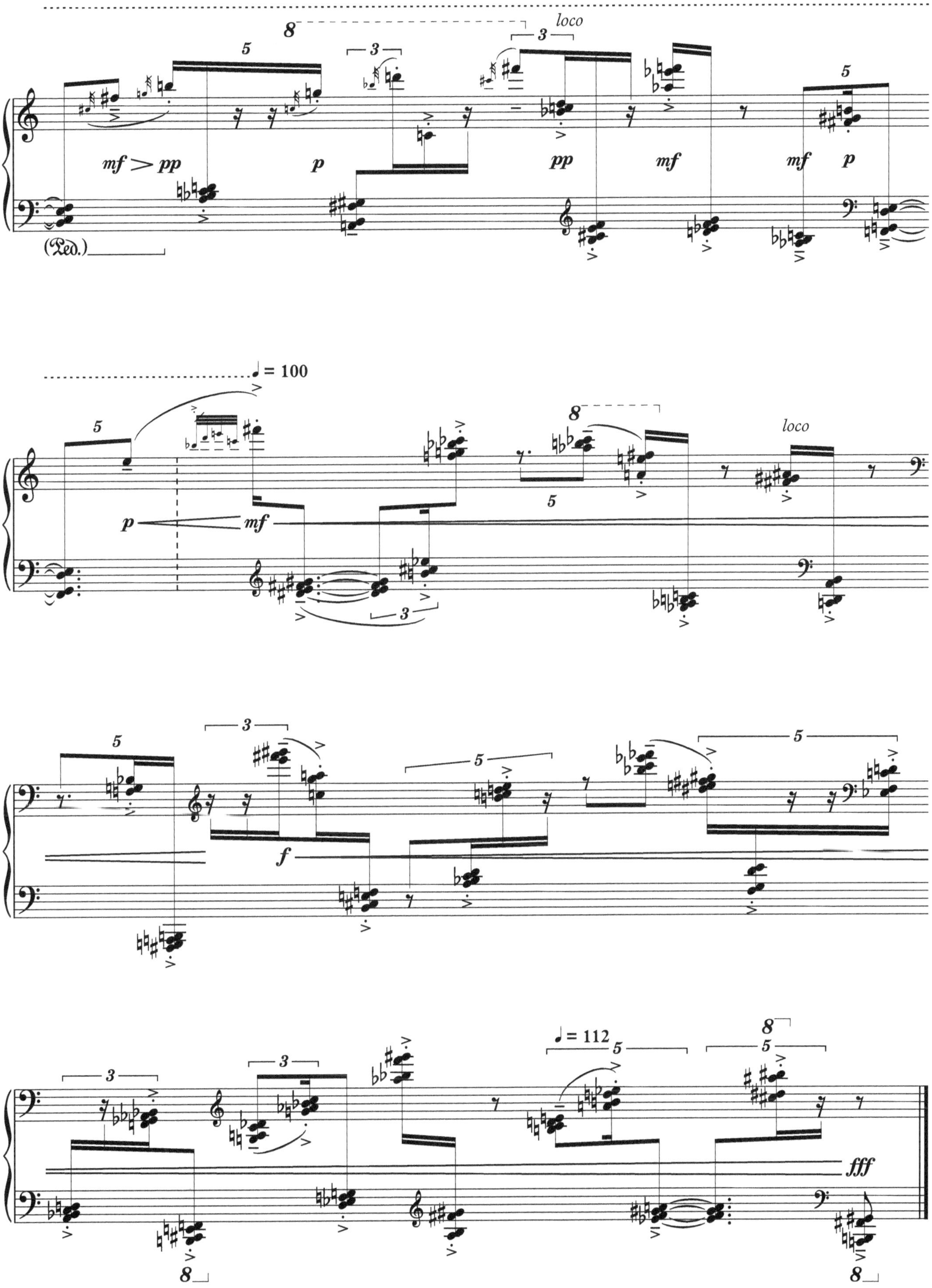
loco
mf > pp
p
pp
mf
(Ped.)
♩ = 100
mf
loco
f
♩ = 112
fff

for Jenny Lin

Etudes for Melancholy Robots:
III. Trains

WILL HEALY
(2018)

♩ = 188
Suddenly slower ♩ = 76
poco rit.
ff
pp sub. , very free
Ped.
Suddenly (♩ = c. 96)
Driving, mechanical (♩ = c. 188)
messy, blurred
ffppp
f
ff sub.
exactly in time
(Ped.)

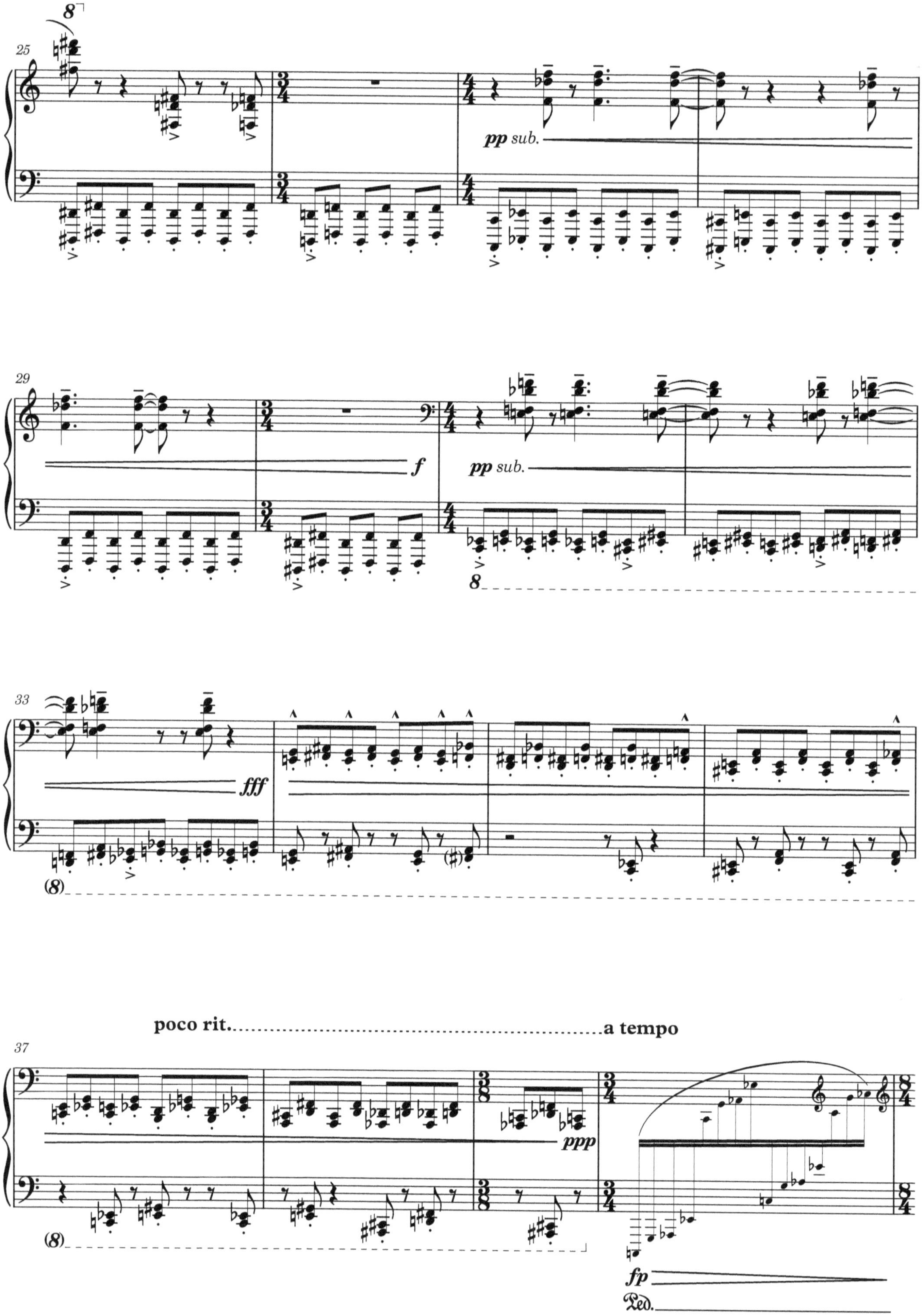
8
25
pp sub.
29
f
pp sub.
8
33
fff
(8)
poco rit.
a tempo
37
ppp
(8)
fp
Ped.

Dark, wandering (♩= c. 96)

freely ★

★ R.H. notes should be free, without any sudden rhythmic changes from one beaming to the next.
L.H. note values guide rhythmic durations
★★ bring out L.H. meoldy

poco rit.

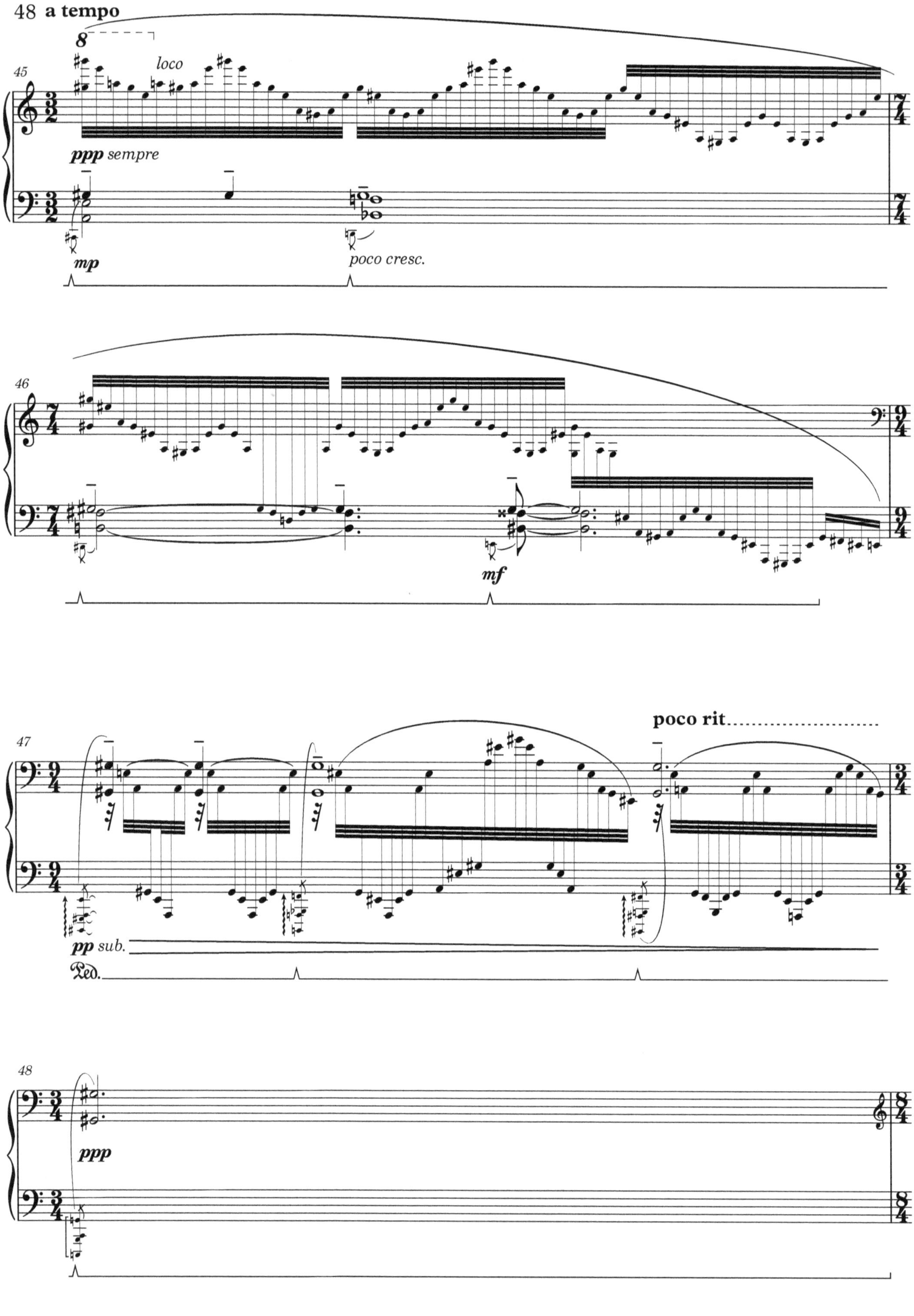
a tempo
8
loco
45
ppp sempre
mp
poco cresc.
46
mf
47
poco rit
pp sub.
Ped.
48
ppp

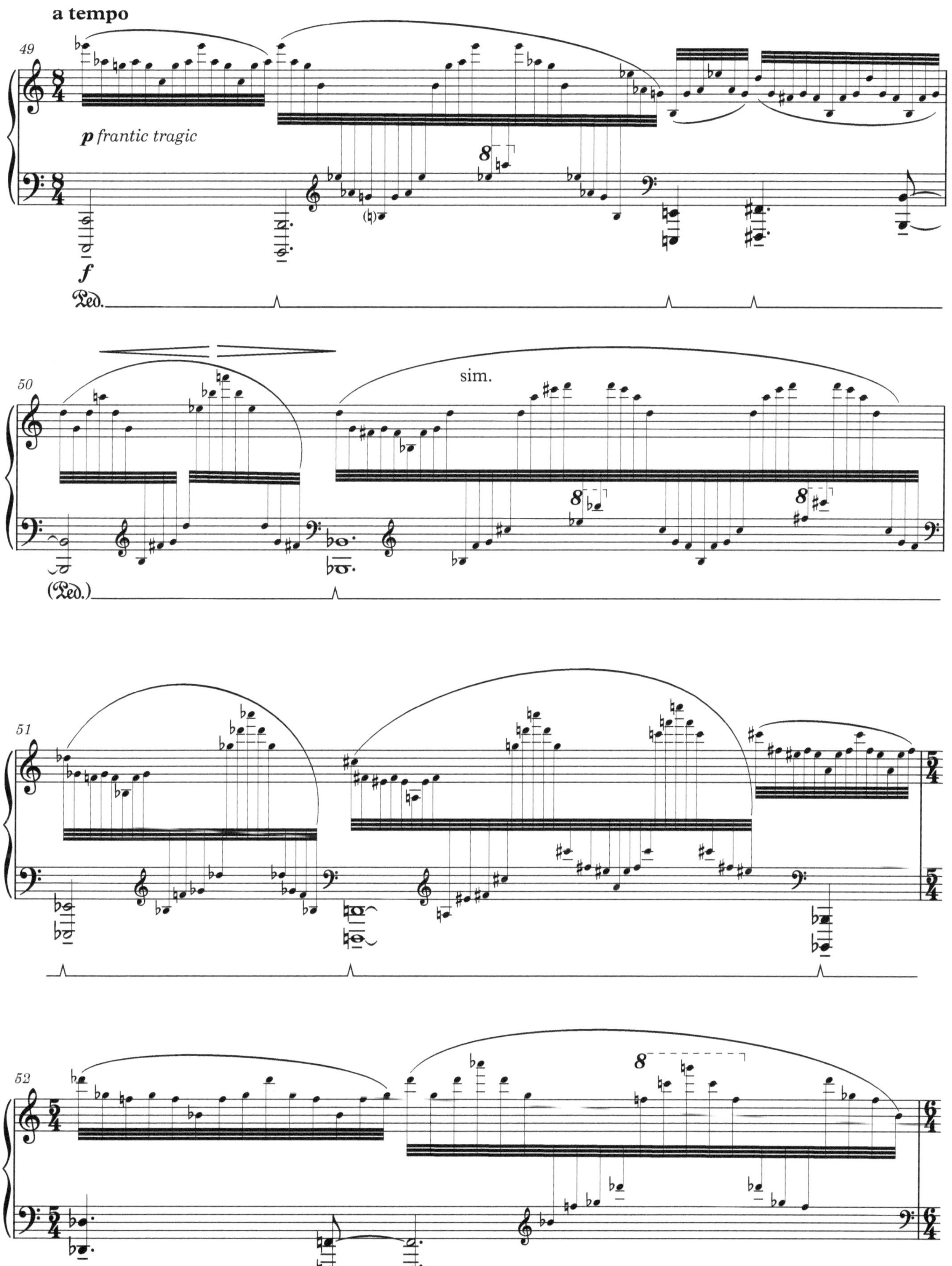
a tempo
49
p frantic tragic
8
f
Ped.
50
sim.
8
8
(Ped.)
51
52
8

molto
53
8
♩ = 110
54
ffpp
steady...
rit.
56
ffpp
Mechanical, percussive (♩ = c. 188)
58
fff sub.
secco

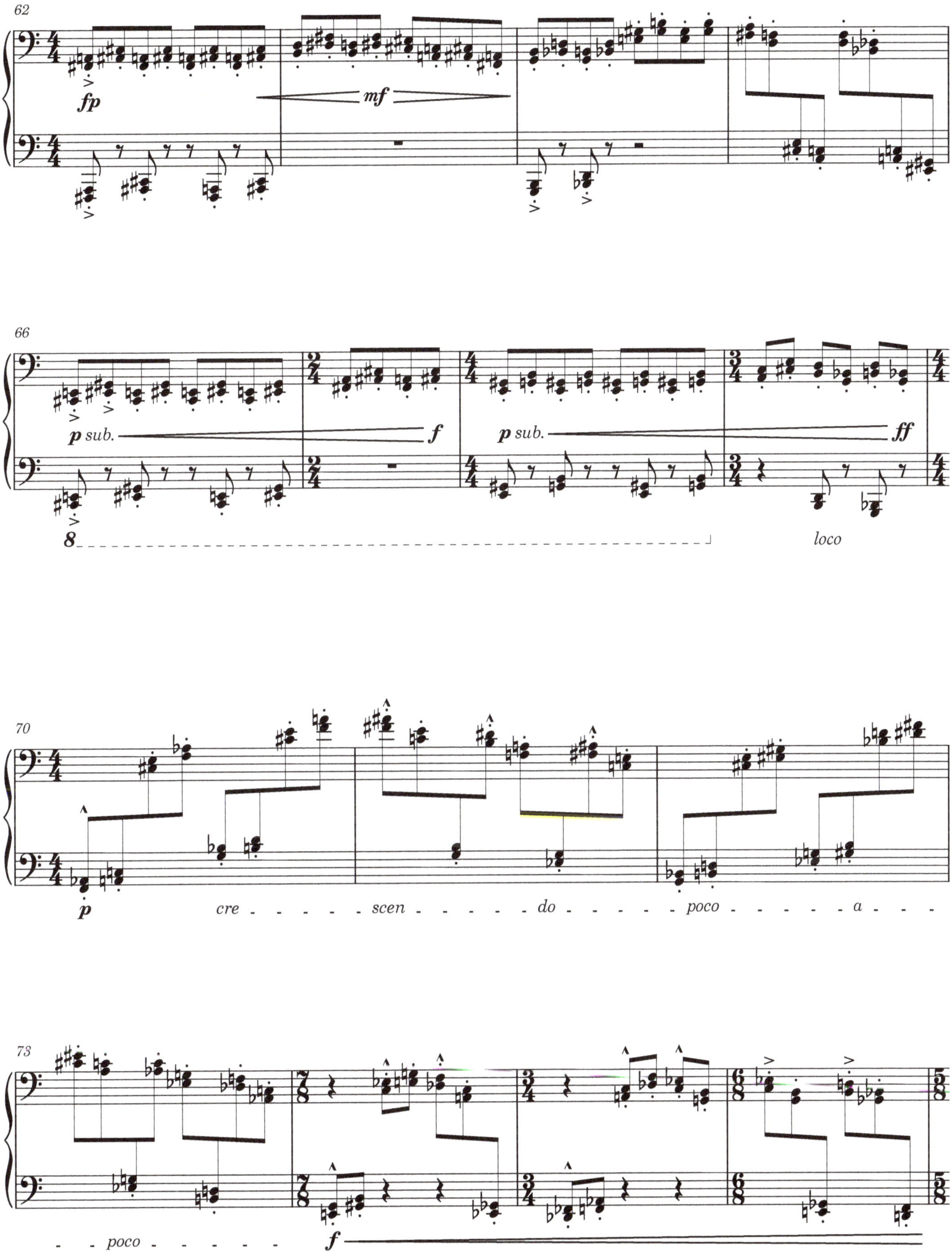
62
fp
mf
66
p sub.
f
p sub.
ff
8
loco
70
p
cre
scen
do
poco
a
73
poco
f

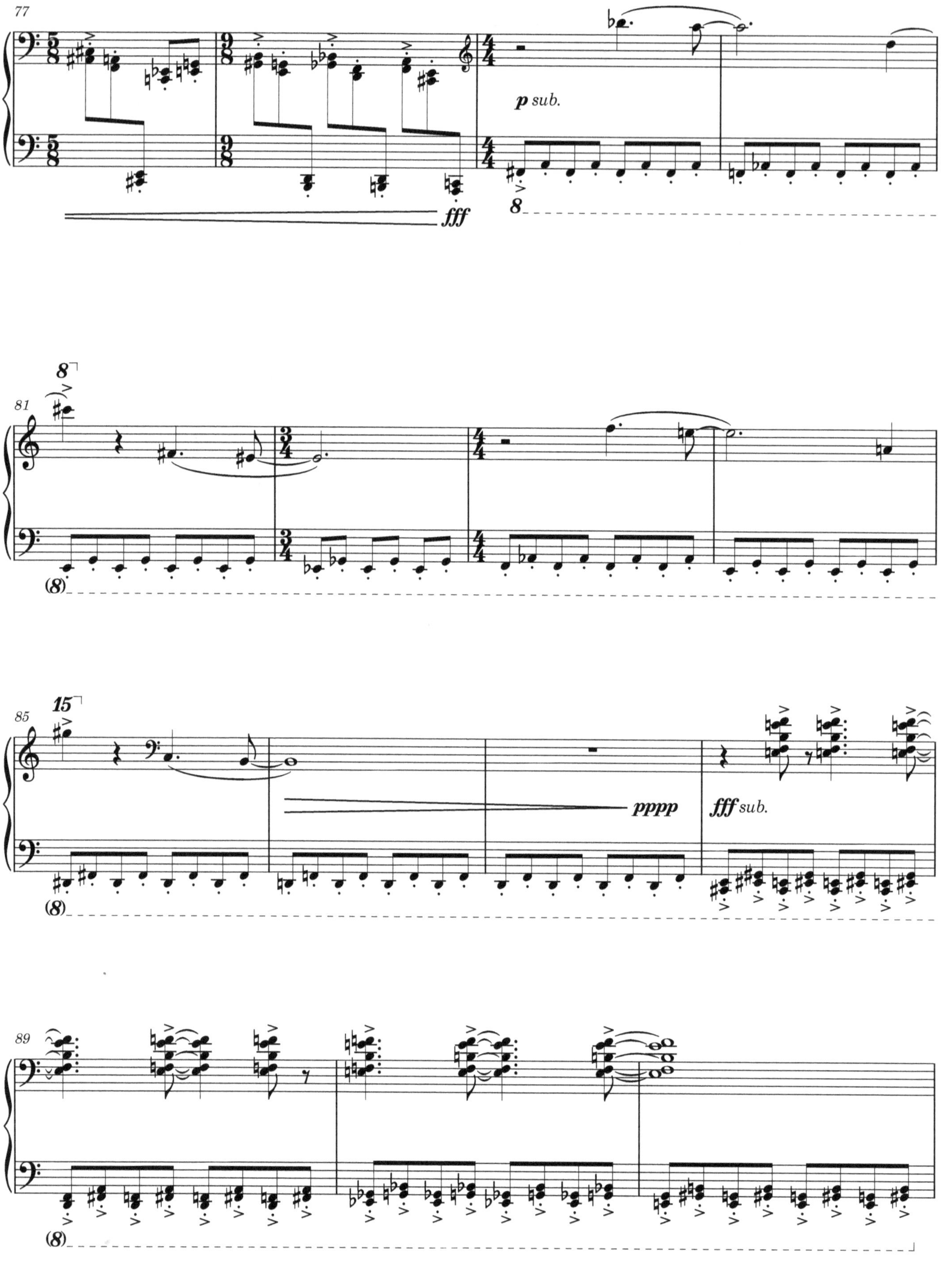
77
fff
p sub.
8
81
8
(8)
85
15
pppp
fff sub.
(8)
89
(8)

Freely, a little slower

(pedal ad lib.)

loco

poco rit. . . . . **Relentless (a tempo)**

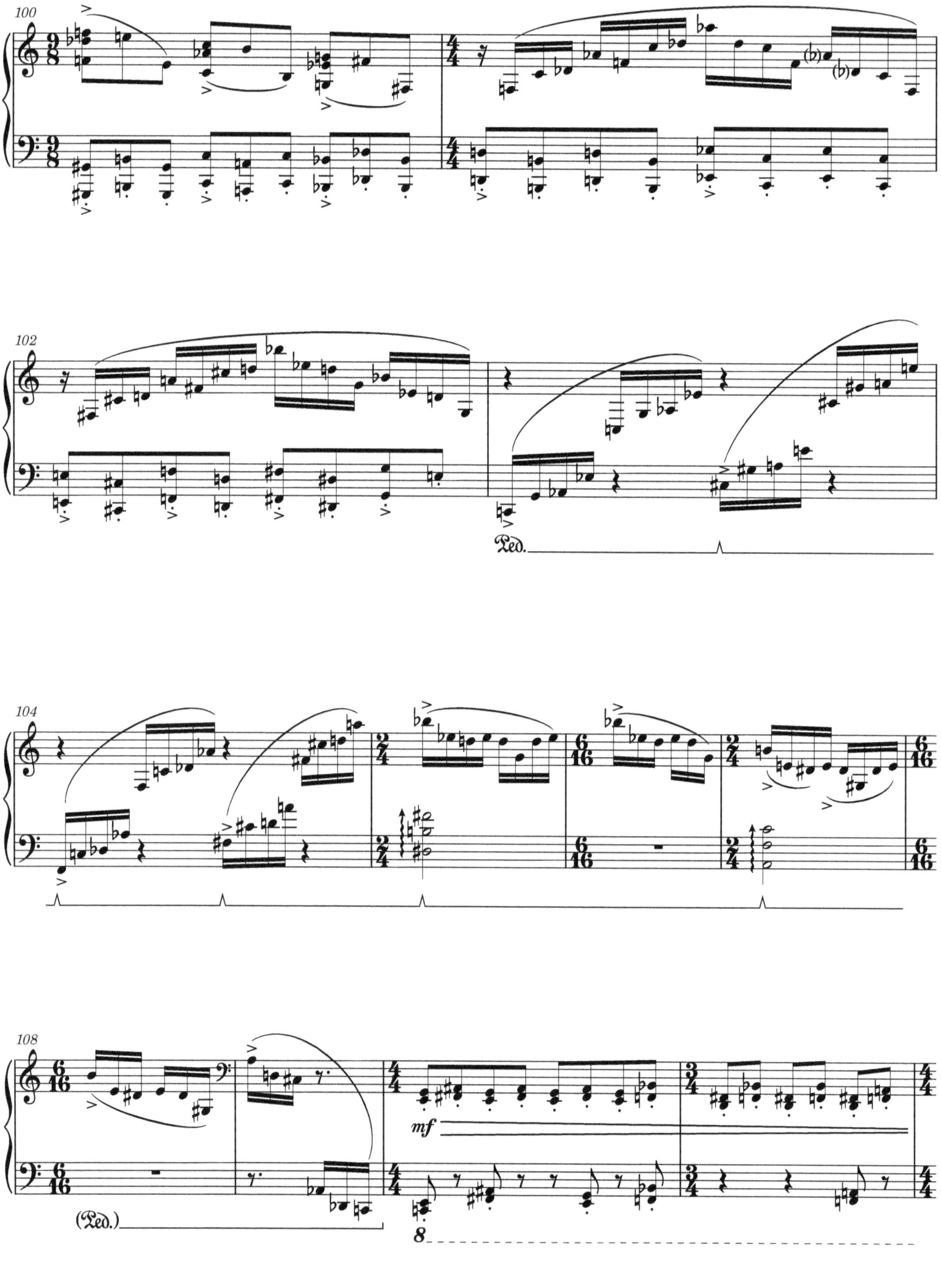
100
102
Ped.
104
108
(Ped.)
mf
8

molto rit. ....

comically slow...

composed for Jenny Lin and ICEBERG New Music

Knuckles

for solo piano

JONATHAN RUSS
(2018)

Deep groove, in strict time (♩ = 116)

f sempre

no pedal

dry and even throughout

mp

f sub.

13
16
soft and warm
p sub.
Ped. Sost., pedal freely
19
slow crescendo to m. 34
22
25
mf cresc.

Ped. Sost. optional

hard beat

f sempre

no pedal

loco

loco

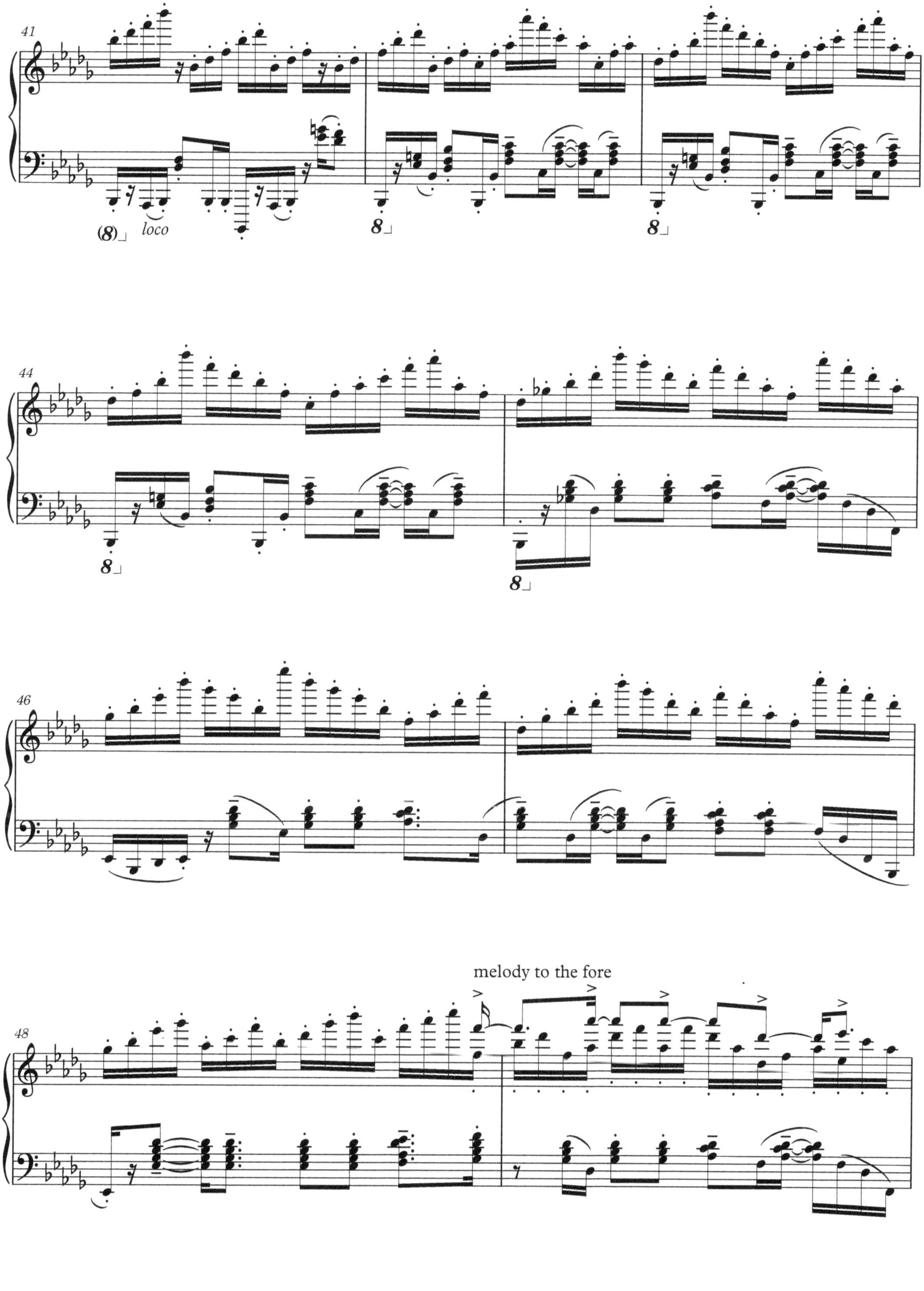
41
(8)
loco
8
8
44
8
8
46
48
melody to the fore

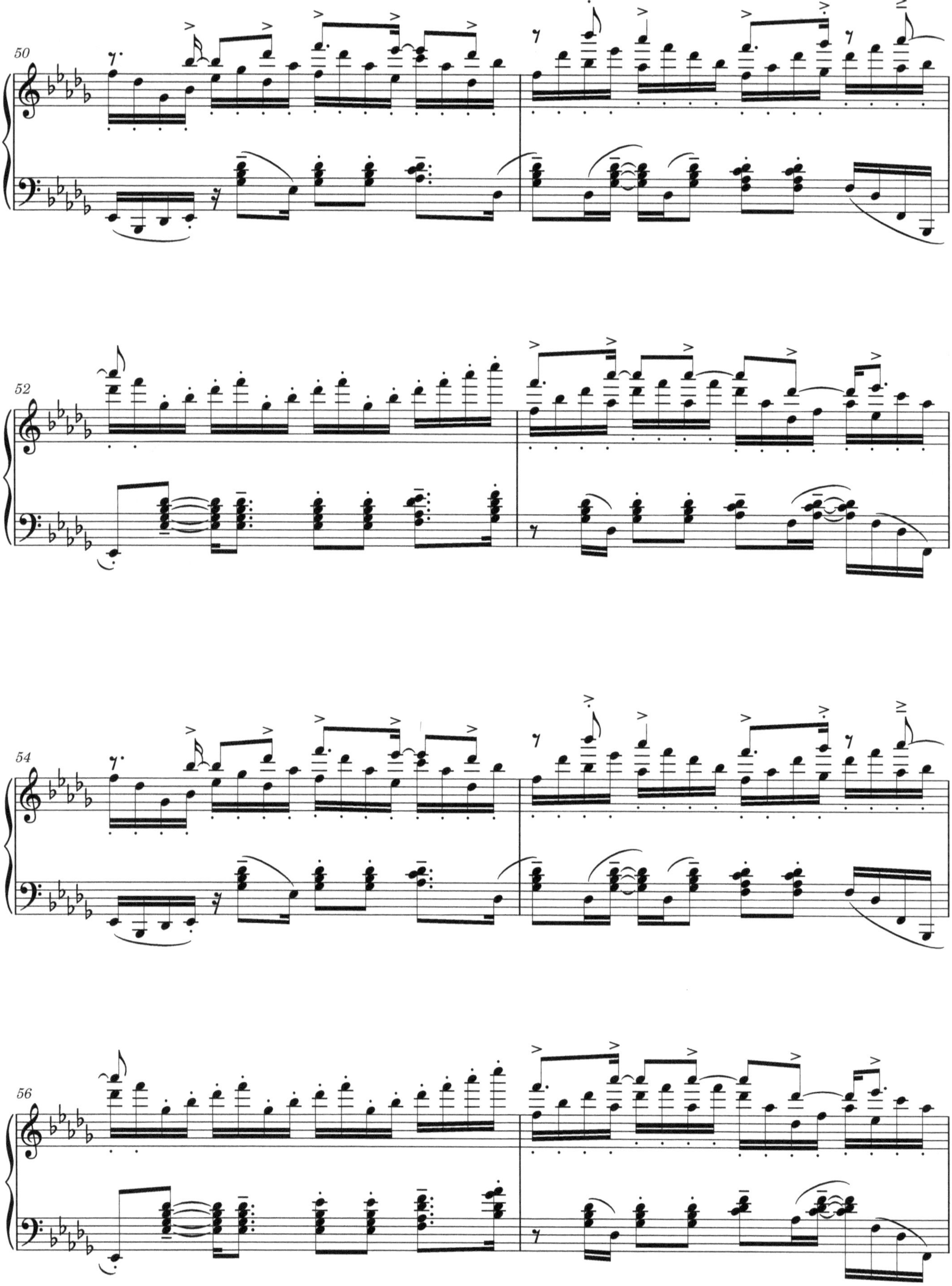
50
52
54
56

warm and joyful

69
cresc.
fluid, like liquid metal
72
sparkly pop
molto
ff
pedal freely
74
8
loco
76
8
loco
8
harsh and heavy, synth-like

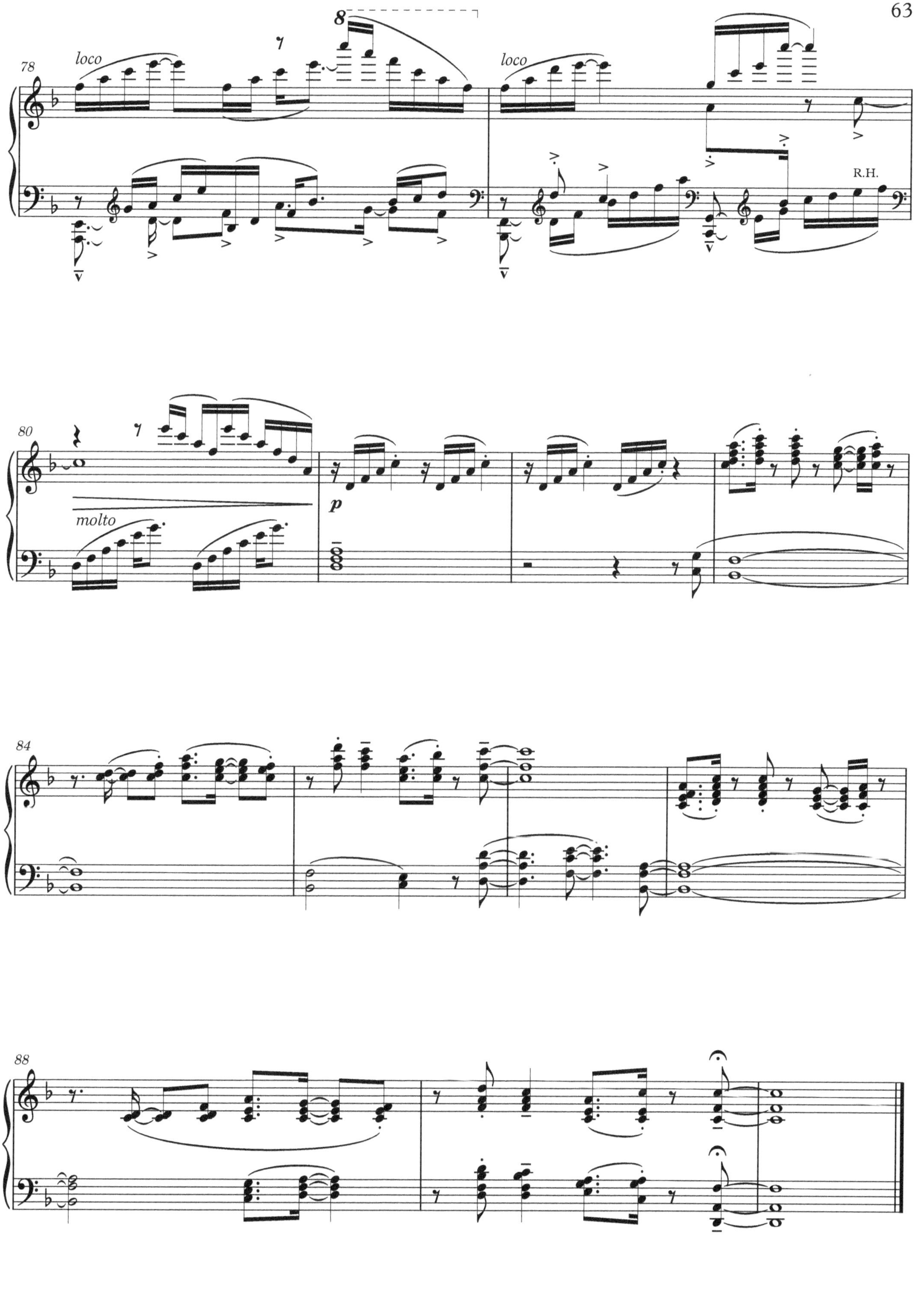
78
loco
8
loco
R.H.
80
molto
p
84
88

to Jenny Lin

Obstinata 1: Barbed Wire

from Piano Études, Book I

HARRY STAFYLAKIS
(2018)

Tempo I: Propulsive (♩ = 120)

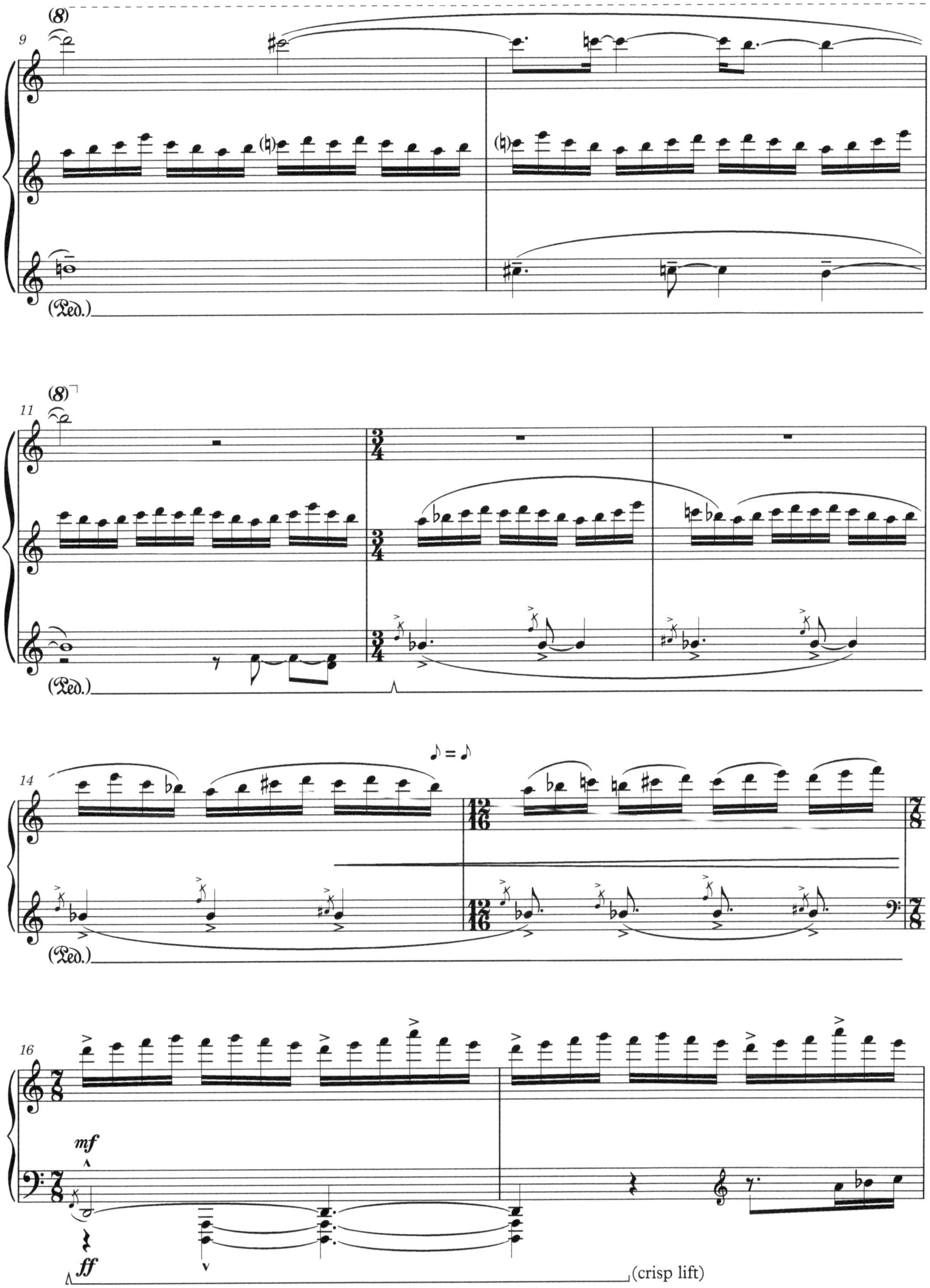
(8)
(Ped.)
(8)
(Ped.)
(Ped.)
mf
ff
(crisp lift)

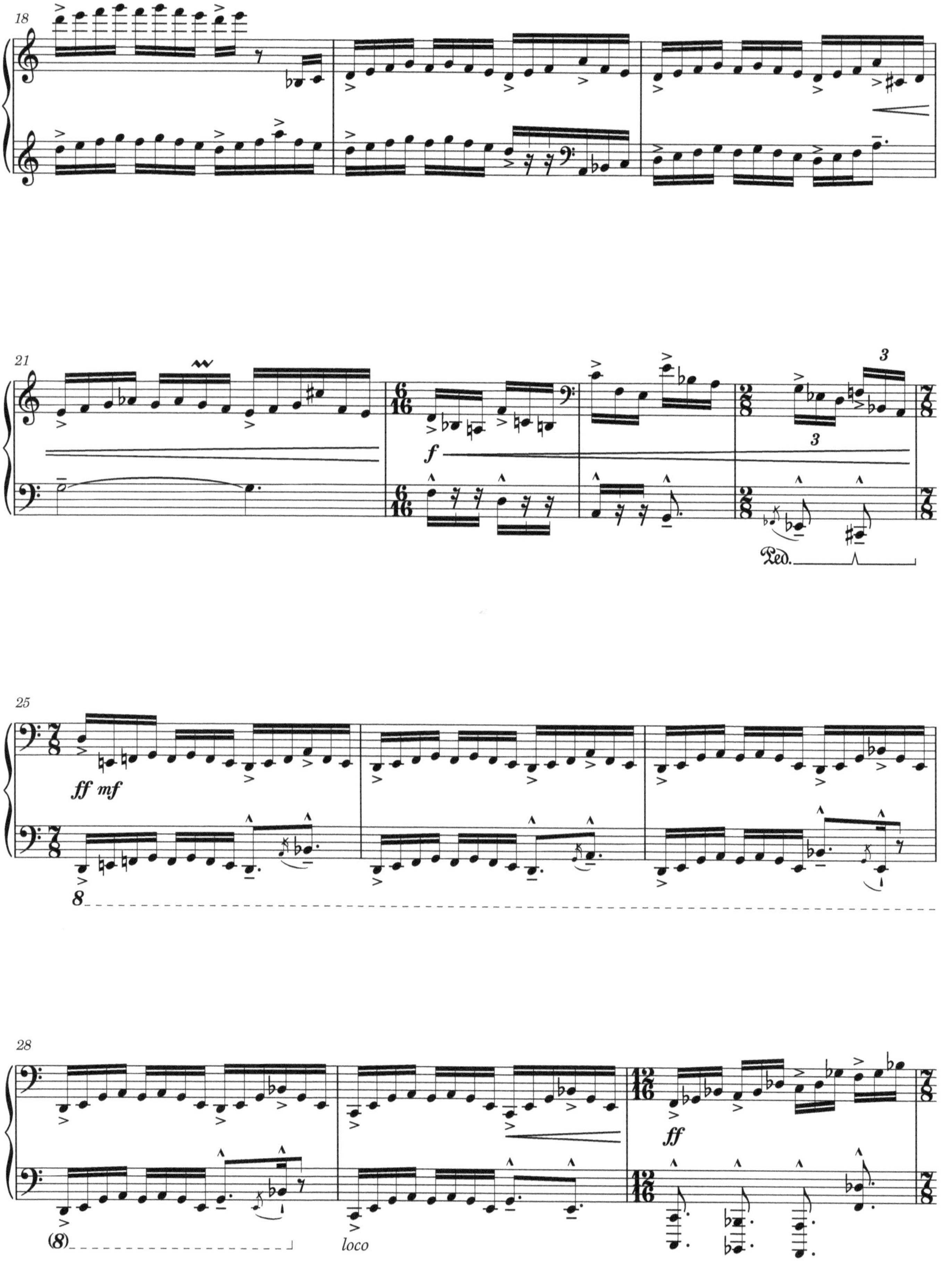
18
21
f
3
Ped.
25
ff mf
8
28
(8)
loco
ff

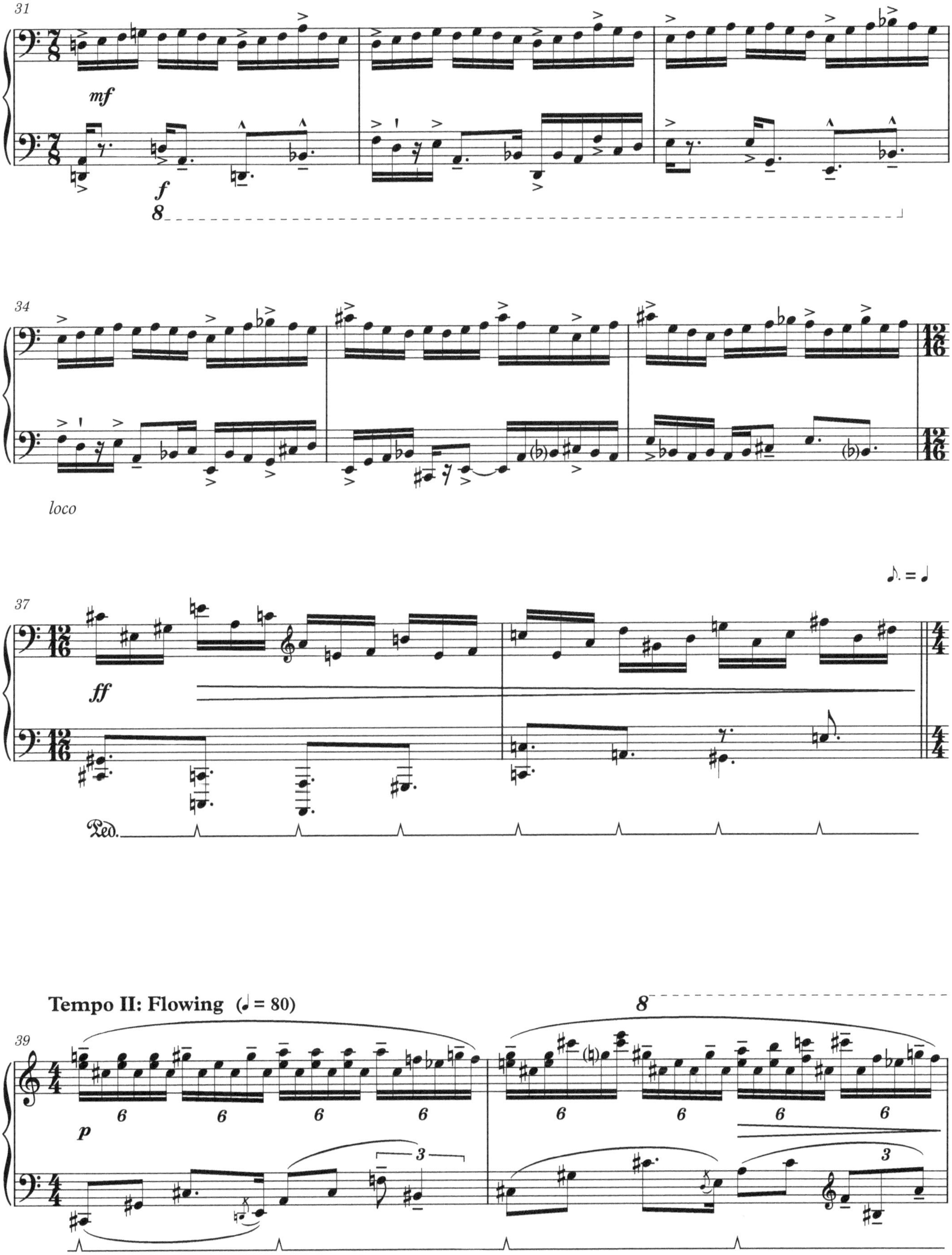
31
mf
f
8
34
loco
37
ff
Ped.
Tempo II: Flowing (♩ = 80)
39
p
8

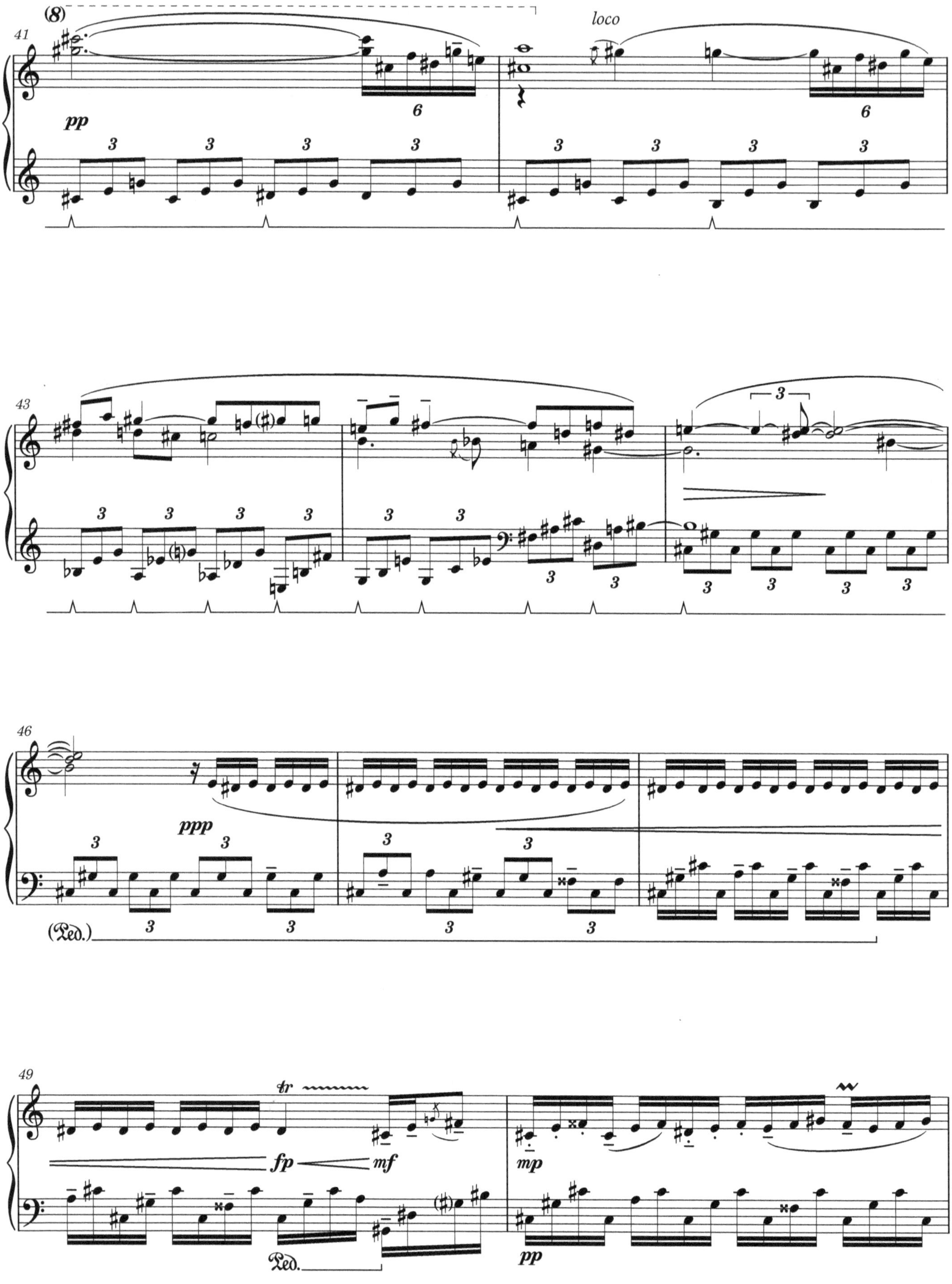
(8)
loco
pp
ppp
(Ped.)
tr
fp
mf
mp
Ped.
pp

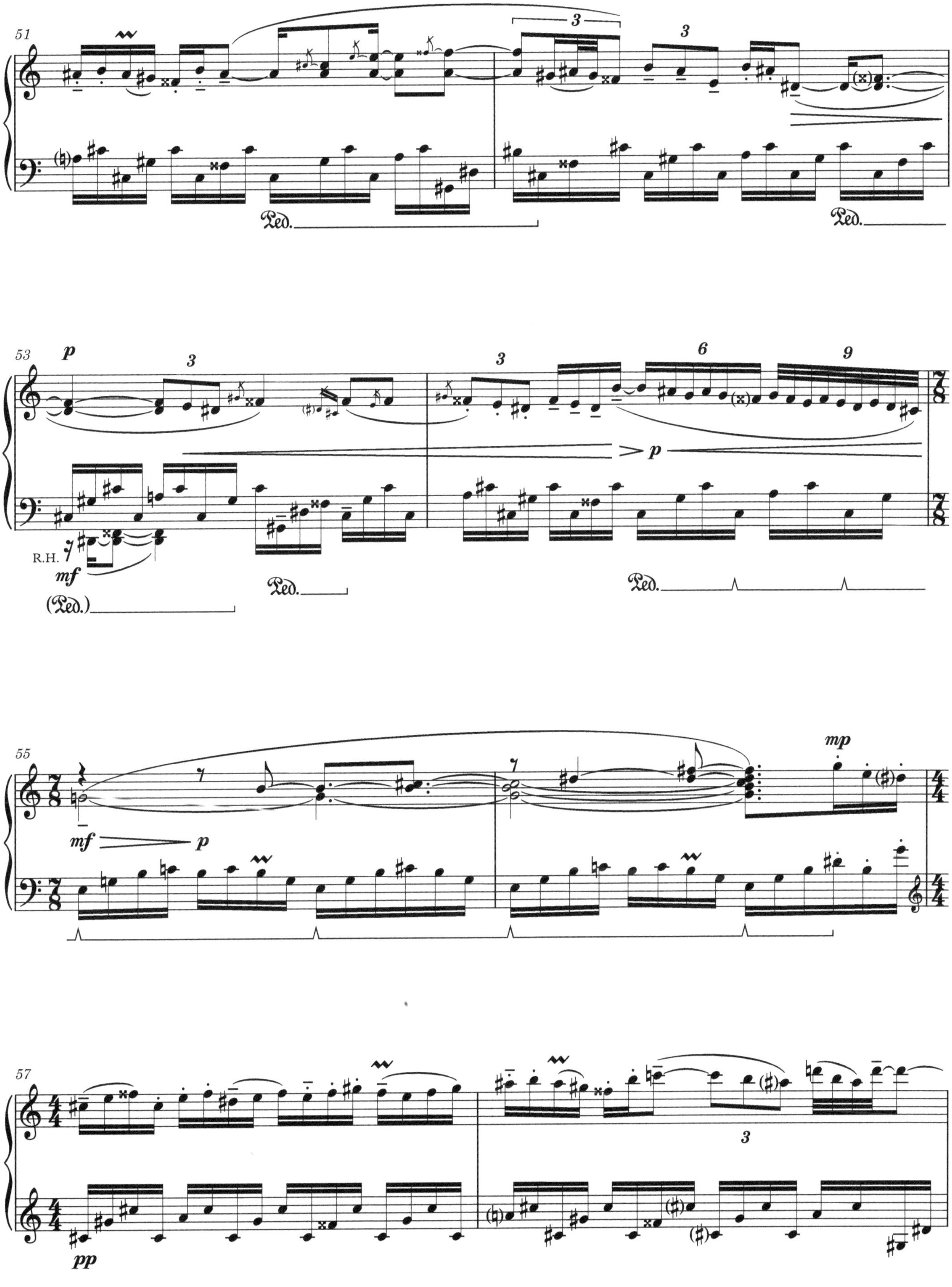
51
3
3
Ped.
Ped.
53
p
3
R.H.
mf
(Ped.)
Ped.
3
6
9
p
Ped.
55
mf
p
mp
57
3
pp

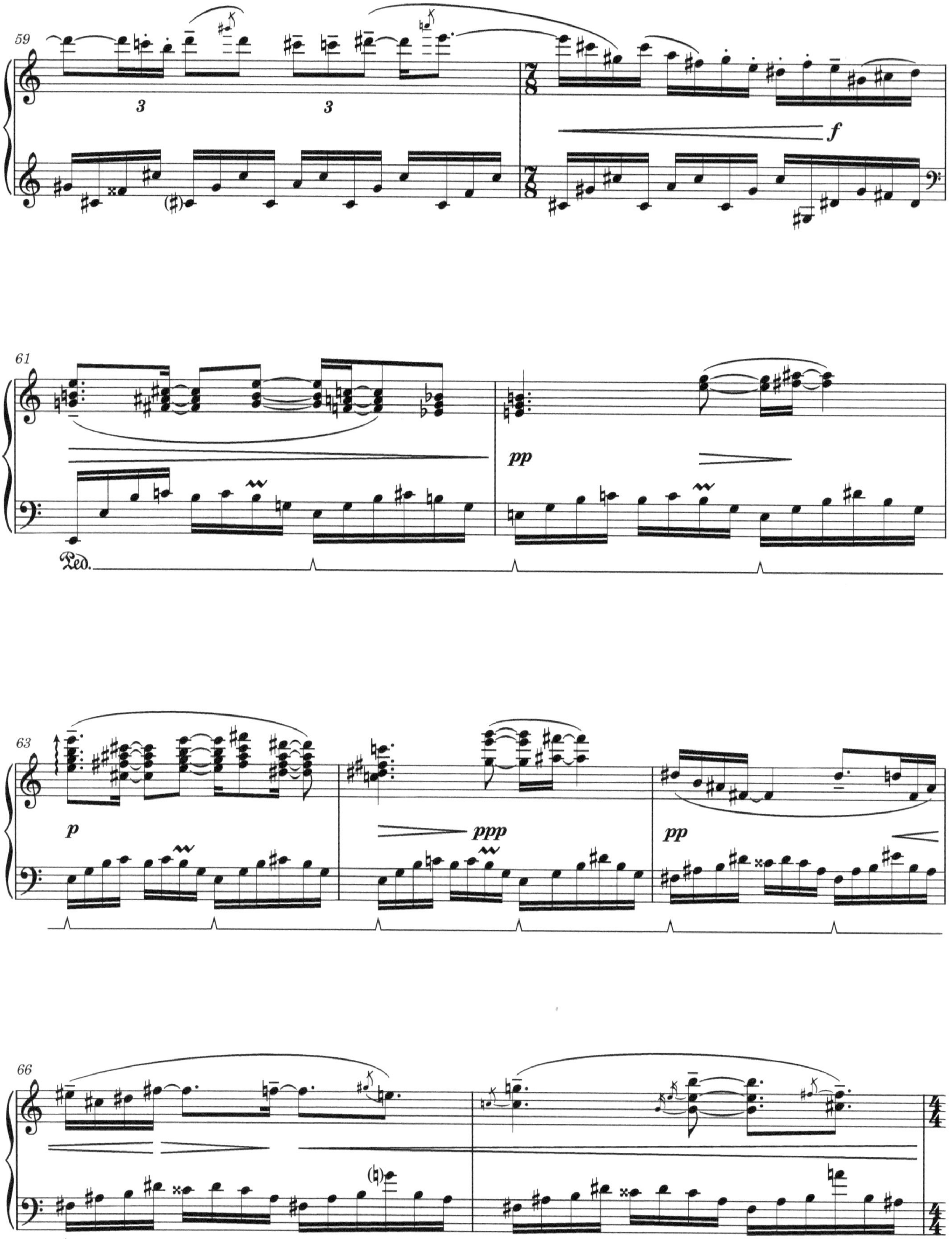
59
3
3
f
61
pp
Ped.
63
p
ppp
pp
66

poco rit.
Freely (♩ = c. 72)
68
mf
ppp
70
pp
poco accel.
73
p
Tempo II: Flowing (♩ = 80)
76
mf

accel. ....

(accelerate Tempo II until it matches Tempo I)

♪ = ♪

détaché

Tempo I: Propulsive (♩ = 120)

Ped.

ff mf

8

(8)

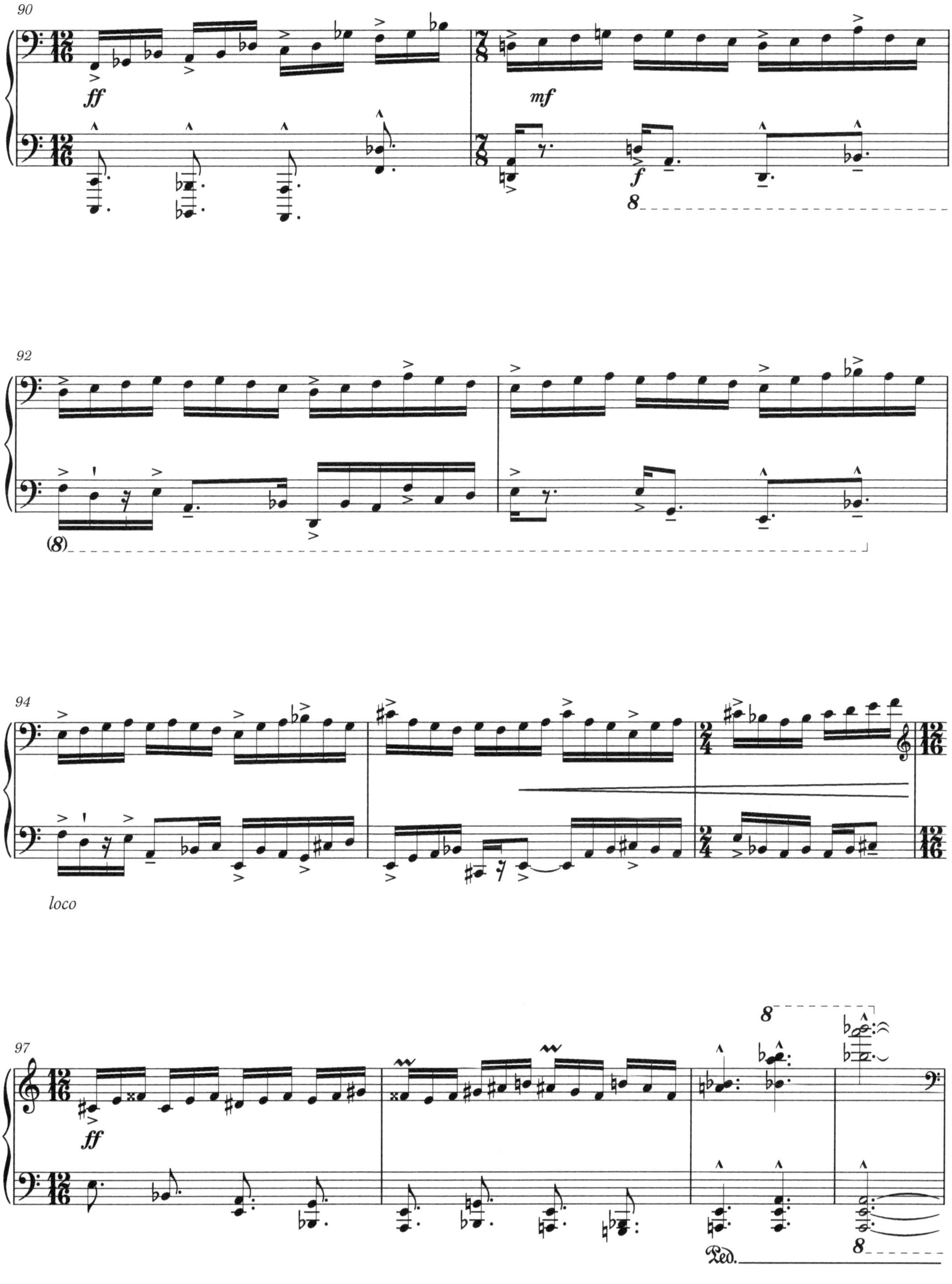
90
ff
mf
f
8
92
(8)
94
loco
97
ff
8
8
Ped.

101

pppp ————————————————————— *f*

(8) -

(Ped.) —————————————————————

Brutal, mechanical (♩ = 120)

103

f

ff

8 - - - - - - - - - - - - - - - - 8 - - - - - - - - - - - - - - - - 8 - - - - - - - -

105

(8) - - - - - - - - - - - - - - - 8 - - - - - - - - - - - - - - - - 8 - - - - - - - -

107

(8) - - - - - - - - - - - - - - - 8 - - - - - - - - - - - - - - - - 8 - - - - - - - -

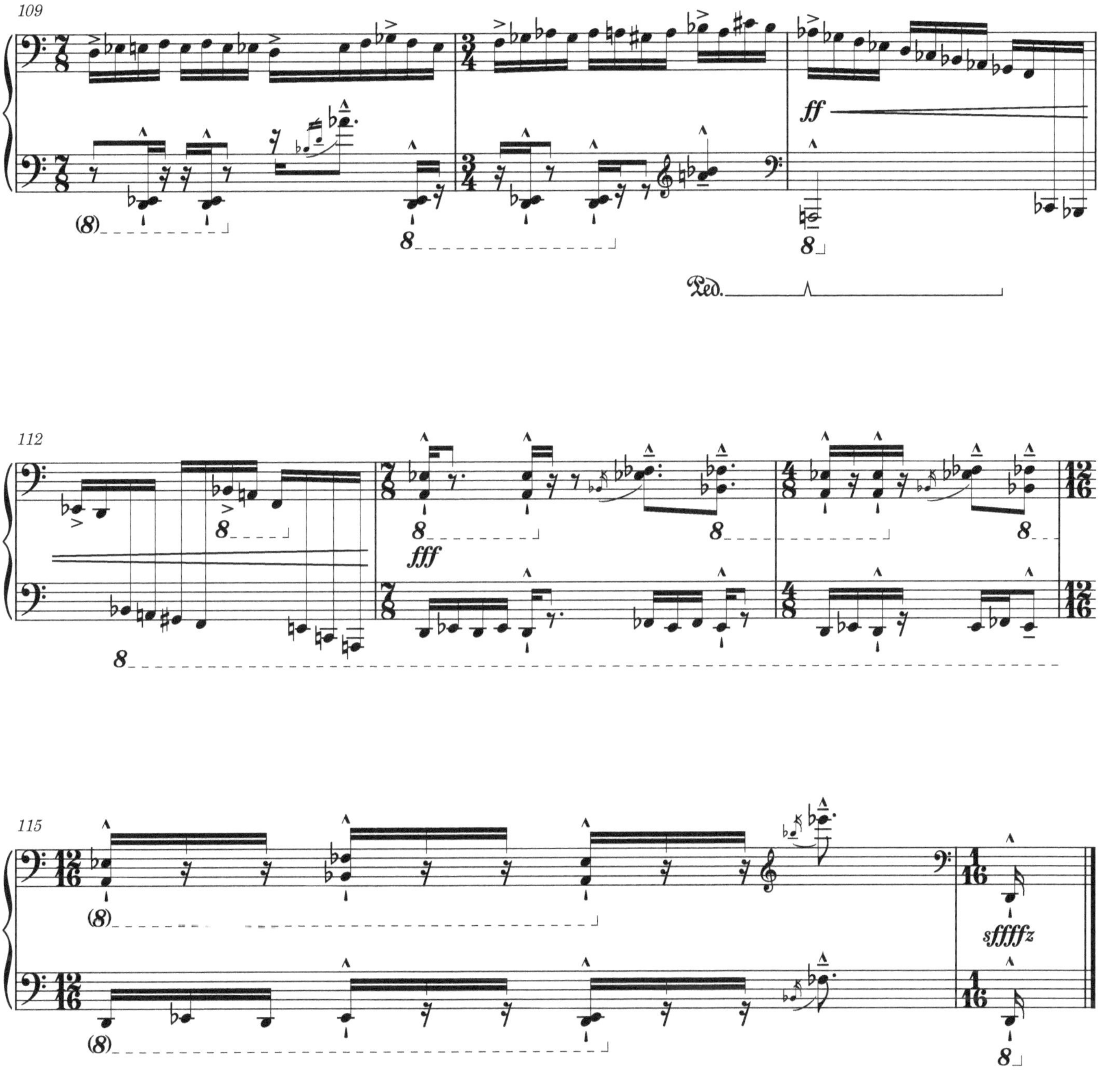
109
(8)
8
8
ff
Ped.
112
8
8
8
fff
8
115
(8)
sffffz
(8)
8

ABOUT THE CURATOR
Jenny Lin

www.jennylin.net

Jenny Lin is one of the most respected young pianists today, admired for her adventurous programming and charismatic stage presence. She has been acclaimed for her "remarkable technical command" and "a gift for melodic flow" by The New York Times. The Washington Post praises "Lin's confident fingers… spectacular technique… ", "…surely one of the most interesting pianists in America right now…" and Gramophone Magazine has hailed her as "an exceptionally sensitive pianist". Her orchestral engagements have included the American Symphony Orchestra, NDR and SWR German Radio orchestras, and Orchestra Sinfonica Nationale della RAI. Her concerts have taken her to Carnegie Hall, Avery Fisher Hall, Kennedy Center, Lincoln Center's Great Performers, SF Jazz, MoMA, Stanford LIVE, and National Gallery of Art, appearing at Festivals such as Mostly Mozart, BAM's Next Wave, Spoleto USA, Kings Place London, Chopin Festival Austria, and Schleswig-Holstein Festival Germany.

Since 2000, Jenny's discography includes more than 30 recordings on Steinway & Sons, Hänssler Classic, eOne, BIS, New World and Albany Records. She is also the central figure in "Cooking for Jenny" by Elemental Films, a musical documentary portraying her journey to Spain. Other media appearances include CBS Sunday Morning, NPR Performance Today, and "Speaking for Myself", a film about Manhattan as seen through the eyes of eight contemporary artists by filmmaker Bert Shapiro. Born in Taiwan and raised in Austria, Jenny studied at the Hochschule für Musik in Vienna, the Peabody Conservatory in Baltimore and the Fondazione Internazionale per il pianoforte in Como, Italy. She holds a bachelor's degree in German literature from The Johns Hopkins University.

Highlights of the 2019/20 season include performances throughout North America and Europe; her continuing "Melody's Mostly Musical Day" children's concerts; the release of the complete piano music of Artur Schnabel, *Etudes Project Volume One*, and music of Philip Glass. Since 2014, she has joined Mr. Glass in his ongoing world tour of his Etudes. Jenny is a Steinway Artist.

About the Composers

Drake Andersen (ASCAP)

b. 1987

drake@drakeandersen.com
www.drakeandersen.com

Drake Andersen is a composer and improviser whose work encompasses acoustic and electro-acoustic music for diverse performing forces of all sizes, collaborative projects for dance and theater, and interactive electronic environments. His music often incorporates improvisation, live electronics, and virtual scores. His compositions have been performed at venues throughout the United States and Europe, including Symphony Space, New World Symphony Center, (le) poisson rouge, and the Park Avenue Armory by artists such as Jenny Lin, Mivos Quartet, and Contemporaneous.

Victor Báez (BMI)

b. 1985

victor.baez.baez@gmail.com
www.victorbaez.com

Born in Mexico City, Víctor Báez is currently based in NYC and Europe. His music has been performed in festivals such as Klangspuren Schwaz, Wien Modern, OME Phoenix, Crosstown Arts Memphis, reMusik in Russia and the International Forum for New Music in Mexico City. He has worked with ensembles such as Yarn/Wire, Ekmeles, Makrokosmos, Contemporaneous, Blueshift, Webern Symphony Orchestra, and others. His works are broadcasted regularly by the Mexican and Austrian radio (Ö1), and his film music has been heard by international audiences in film festivals across the globe.

A Fulbright Scholar, his awards include 6 consecutive yearly Composition Grants from the Austrian Ministry of Arts, Culture and Education, a START Grant for Young Artists from the Austrian government, and a Grant for Artistic Studies Abroad from the Mexican National Arts Fund (Fonca).

As an educator, he maintains an ongoing relationship as Visiting Professor with the Barenboim-Said Foundation in Ramallah, Palestine.

Professionally, his main interest is to collaborate with musicians and other artists towards the realization of creative projects that will pose an interesting question or challenge – both to the artists and the audience involved.

Stephanie Ann Boyd (ASCAP)

b. 1990

www.stephanieannboyd.com

Michigan-born American composer Stephanie Ann Boyd (b. 1990) writes melodic music about women's memoirs and the natural world for symphonic and chamber ensembles. Her work has been performed in nearly all 50 states and has been commissioned by musicians and organizations in 37 countries. Boyd's five ballets include works choreographed by New York City Ballet principal dancers Lauren Lovette, Ashley Bouder, NYCB soloist Peter Walker, and XOAC Contemporary Ballet's Eryn Renee Young. *Eero*, a ballet commissioned by Access Contemporary Music and Open House New York, was written for the grand opening of the TWA Hotel at JFK Airport. Stephanie's music has been praised as "[with] ethereal dissonances" (*Boston Globe*), "[music that] didn't let itself be eclipsed" (*Texas Classical Review*), "arrestingly poetic" (*BMOP*), and "wide ranging, imaginative" (*Portland Press Herald*).

Stephanie was the 2016-18 Composer in Residence for the Eureka Ensemble in Boston, the 2013/14 Collage New Music Fellow, and has had composition residencies at summer festivals in Italy, Canada, and the US. Boyd has taught composition privately for eight years and her students have been accepted into the music schools at University of Toronto, University of Michigan, Indiana University, UC Boulder, Michigan State University, and others. She is a recipient of the Donald Martino Award for Excellence in Composition and is a two-time recipient of the CCPA Vector Award, and has won numerous grants from the Women's Philharmonic Advocacy. She holds degrees from Roosevelt University and New England Conservatory (with honors). Boyd was one of the last violin students of renowned pedagogue John Kendall.

Boyd is a member of the Iceberg New Music Composers Collective. Her catalog is published by TRN Music and FEMOIRE. A critic for American Record Guide and I Care If You Listen, Boyd lives in Manhattan. She is often dressed by Michelle Smith of MILLY for concerts and events and this season her red carpet and gala outfits are by Boston designer Sasha Parfenova.

Alex Burtzos (ASCAP)

b. 1985

alexburtzosmusic@gmail.com
www.alexburtzosmusic.com

Alex Burtzos is an American composer and conductor based in New York City and Orlando, FL. His work has been performed across four continents. Alex has collaborated with some of the world's foremost contemporary musicians and ensembles, including JACK Quartet, Yarn/Wire, Contemporaneous, ETHEL, loadbang, Jenny Lin, RighteousGIRLS, and many others. He is the founder and artistic director of ICEBERG New Music, a New Yorkbased composers' collective, and the conductor of the hip-hop/classical chamber orchestra ShoutHouse.

As a composer, Alex is committed to pursuing artistic expression unconstrained by boundaries of school or style. His music often incorporates elements of the 20th Century avant-garde, jazz, rock, metal, and hip-hop alongside or against classical/preclassical structures and sounds, justifying these juxtapositions with a great depth of musical ideas and extra-musical knowledge. Alex's music takes as its basis and provides commentary on a diverse array of subject matter, from early colonial history to recent events, from Shakespeare's tragedies to naughty text messages. His unique approach has earned him accolades and awards from organizations around the world.

Alex holds a DMA from Manhattan School of Music, where his primary teachers were Reiko Fueting and Mark Stambaugh. He is Chair of Composition Studies at The University of Central Florida.

Yu-Chun Chien

b. 1987

www.yuchunchien.com

Yu-Chun Chien is a Taiwanese composer based in the United States and Taiwan. Her compositions and arrangements have been published and performed in Taiwan, the United States, Germany, France, Finland, Italy and the Netherlands. She has appeared at festivals and residencies such as Time of Music (Musiikin aika), ilSUONO Contemporary Music Week, June in Buffalo, Internationales Musikinstitut Darmstadt, impuls International Ensembles and Composers Academy for Contemporary Music, Asian Composers League Conference and Festival, Etchings Festival, and the Loretto Project.

Yu-Chun Chien has received several prizes, awards, scholarships, grants and commissions, including the Second Prize, the Orchestra's Choice and the Audience's Choice in the Orchestra Composition Competitions held by the National Taiwan Symphony Orchestra, the Distinction Awards in the Solo/Duet Composition Competition and Choral Composition Competition organized by the National Chiang Kai-Shek Cultural Center, the Representative Piece in the Asian Composers League Conference and Festival, the "Call for Score" Commission Award from the National Taiwan Symphony Orchestra, the Scholarship for Overseas Study from the Ministry of Education in Taiwan, the Grants from the National Culture and Arts Foundation, and Nina Elizabeth Nilssen Scholarship Fund.

Yu-Chun Chien is a Visiting Assistant Professor at West Virginia University. Previously, she was appointed coordinator of aural skills and coordinator of theory tutoring program at Manhattan School of Music.

Yu-Chun Chien received her Doctor of Musical Arts and Master of Music degrees from Manhattan School of Music in New York, and her Bachelor of Music degree from Taipei National University of the Arts in Taiwan. Some of her most influential teachers have been Reiko Füting, Susan Botti and Chung-Kun Hung.

As a composer, Yu-Chun Chien constantly searches for new means of expression, which can be transformed in personal and intimate ways.

Derek Cooper (BMI)

b. 1987

DACooperMusic@gmail.com
www.DerekCooperComposer.com

Derek Cooper's music has been performed worldwide by groups including Contemporaneous, Sonic Apricity, the Indiana University of Pennsylvania wind ensemble, Jenny Lin, Yarn/Wire, Ekmeles, the Iridium Saxophone Quartet, and Blueshift Ensemble. His piece, Kill James, was recently awarded an honorable mention for the New York Composers Circle's 2019 Joh Eaton Memorial Composition Competition. In 2016, Derek joined the ICEBERG collective, a select and diverse group of emerging New York composers.

Earning his Bachelor's degree in Music Theory and Composition in 2009 from Indiana University of Pennsylvania, Derek studied with American Prix de Rome winner Daniel Perlongo while also taking lessons with Jack Stamp, Christopher Marshal, and Richard Danielpour. Derek continued to study with Richard Danielpour, earning his Master's degree from Manhattan School of Music in composition in 2014. In the Fall of 2014, Derek returned to Manhattan School of Music to begin his doctoral studies under Dr. Reiko Fueting as a doctoral teaching fellow.

Derek currently teaches music theory at Ramapo College of New Jersey's School of Contemporary Arts as well as teaching composition and musicianship courses at the Hoff-Barthelson Music School. He also teaches theory and ear training at Manhattan School of Music and during the summer, he oversees the composition department for MSM Summer. His music is published through his own website as well as Knightwind Music and NewMusicShelf. For more information and to hear samples of Derek's work, visit: www.DerekCooperComposer.com.

Max Grafe (ASCAP)

b. 1988

www.maxgrafe.com

Max Grafe (b. 1988) writes music with the aim of striking a distinctive balance between the stylistic immediacy of modernism and the dramatic power of romanticism. Max's music has been performed by a wide range of prominent and emerging ensembles—including the New York Philharmonic, Contemporaneous, Yarn/Wire, Quince Ensemble, New Thread Quartet, and Flux Quartet—and has been featured at numerous music festivals across the country, including the Tanglewood Music Center, the Resonant Bodies Festival, and the Santa Fe Chamber Music Festival. Upcoming projects include collaborations with Hypercube, hornist Steven Cohen, Duo Entre-Nous, and ensembleNEWSRQ. Max is a founding member of New York-based composer collective Iceberg New Music, which is preparing to launch its fourth season in collaboration with Hypercube and Unheard-of Ensemble. Max's music appears on commercial recordings by the New York Philharmonic, Quince Ensemble, pianist Mika Sasaki, and harpist Emily Levin, and will be featured on multiple upcoming commercial releases, including an album by pianist Jenny Lin of etudes written for her by Iceberg composers.

Max has received several of the most prestigious awards available to emerging American composers, including a Charles Ives Scholarship from the American Academy of Arts and Letters, a William Schuman Prize from BMI, two consecutive Palmer Dixon Prizes from the Juilliard School, and a Morton Gould Young Composer Award from ASCAP. He also once narrowly edged out Dmitri Shostakovich in a Facebook opinion poll of favorite composers, of which he is prouder than he probably should be.

Max is a member of the music faculties at Hofstra University and the Kaufman Music Center. He received a Doctor of Musical Arts degree from the Juilliard School in 2018, a Master of Music degree from Juilliard in 2013 and a Bachelor of Music degree from the Jacobs School of Music at Indiana University in 2011. Further studies have taken place at Mannes College of Music, the Freie Universität Berlin, the Aspen Music Festival and School, and the Tanglewood Music Center.

Will Healy (ASCAP)

b. 1990

wdhealy@gmail.com
www.willhealymusic.com

Will Healy is a composer and pianist based in New York. Noted for his "lushly bluesy" sound and "adroitly blended… textures" (*New York Times*), he is the artistic director of ShoutHouse, a collective of hip-hop, jazz, and classical musicians. After playing trumpet in an Afrobeat band for a few years, he grew interested in collaborating with performers from many corners of the New York music scene. In addition, he is an accomplished pianist specializing in Bach, with a repertoire that includes the complete *Goldberg Variations*. Healy was the recipient of the Richard Rodgers Scholarship at The Juilliard School, where he studied with John Corigliano, Steven Stucky, and Samuel Adler. He has also studied with Kevin Puts, Harold Meltzer, and Richard Wilson.

Recent awards include a Charles Ives Scholarship from the American Academy of Arts and Letters, two ASCAP Morton Gould Awards, the W.K. Rose Fellowship, a JFund commission from the American Composers Forum, and prizes in the Juilliard and Kaleidoscope Orchestra Composition Competitions. He was the recipient of the Aaron Copland Prize from the Bogliasco Foundation in 2018, and has been a fellow at the Aspen Music Festival, Minnesota Orchestra Composers Institute, and the L.A. Phil's National Composers Intensive. Healy's work has appeared at The Kennedy Center, Lincoln Center, The Apollo, on the NY Philharmonic's Biennial series, on "New Sounds" with John Schaefer (WNYC) and "Making Music" (WBAI), and more. He studied piano for many years with Dennis Malone at the Crestwood Music School.

Jonathan Russ (ASCAP)

b. 1985

jon@jonathanrussmusic.com
www.jonathanrussmusic.com

Jon (he/him) writes music. He's been to some schools for it, won a couple awards, worked with some people you may or may not have heard of. He's currently in residence with the American Chamber Ensemble and the Blueshift Ensemble.

Jon likes melody and emotional precision. Other musical interests include the I Ching, Star Trek: Deep Space Nine, Marcel Lapierre Morgon, Chongqing fried chicken, and the New York Islanders. He lives in Bushwick, Brooklyn, NY.

Harry Stafylakis (ASCAP/SOCAN)

b. 1982

info@hstafylakis.com
www.hstafylakis.com

New York City-based composer Harry Stafylakis (b. 1982) hails from Montreal, Canada. "Dreamy yet rhythmic" (*NY Times*), with a "terrible luminosity" and "ferociously expressive" (*Times Colonist*), his concert music is "an amalgamation of the classical music tradition and the soul and grime of heavy metal" (*I Care If You Listen*), "favoring doomsday chords and jackhammer rhythms" (*The New Yorker*).

Stafylakis is the Winnipeg Symphony Orchestra's Composer-In-Residence and Co-Curator of the WSO's Winnipeg New Music Festival. His works have been performed by the Toronto, Winnipeg, Vancouver, Edmonton, Ottawa, Victoria, PEI, Spokane, Stamford, FSU, and Greek Youth Symphony Orchestras, Norwegian Radio Orchestra, American Composers Orchestra, McGill Chamber Orchestra, Roomful of Teeth, JACK Quartet, ICE, Contemporaneous, Mivos Quartet, Quatuor Bozzini, Aspen Contemporary Ensemble, Standing Wave, Paramirabo, Nouveau Classical Project, mise-en, Lorelei Ensemble, and American Modern Ensemble. He has been featured at the NY Philharmonic Biennial, Aspen Music Festival, Winnipeg New Music Festival, and the Montreal International Classical Guitar Festival. In 2019 he collaborated with progressive metal pioneers Animals As Leaders on the orchestral adaptation of their music for metal band & orchestra.

Awards include the Charles Ives Fellowship from the American Academy of Arts and Letters, the ASCAP Foundation's Leonard Bernstein Award, four SOCAN Foundation Awards for Young Composers, and grants from the Canada Council for the Arts, NYSCA, SSHRC, and New Music USA. He serves on the board of directors of GroundSwell (Winnipeg), is an Associate Composer of the Canadian Music Centre, and a founding member of the NYC composer collective ICE-BERG New Music.

Stafylakis holds degrees from McGill University and The Graduate Center, CUNY, and lectures at the City College of New York. His research examines the conception of rhythm and meter in progressive metal.

Supplementary Materials

Texts, program notes, composer biographies, and composer headshots can be found at:

https://newmusicshelf.com/etudes1-info/